DISEASES & DISORDERS

Cholera

Diane Yancey

LUCENT BOOKS
A part of Gale, Cengage Learning

GALE
CENGAGE Learning·

Detroit • New York • San Francisco • New Haven, Conn • Waterville, Maine • London

LIBRARY OF CONGRESS CATALOGING-IN-PUBLICATION DATA

Yancey, Diane.
  Cholera / by Diane Yancey.
    pages cm. -- (Diseases & disorders)
  Includes bibliographical references and index.
  ISBN 978-1-4205-0934-2 (hardcover)
  1. Cholera. 2. Cholera--History. I. Title.
  RC126.Y36 2013
  616.9'32--dc23

                                              2012046618

Lucent Books
27500 Drake Rd.
Farmington Hills, MI 48331

ISBN-13: 978-1-4205-0934-2
ISBN-10: 1-4205-0934-9

Printed in the United States of America
2 3 4 5 6 7 17 16 15 14 13

Table of Contents

"The Most Difficult Puzzles Ever Devised"

Charles Best, one of the pioneers in the search for a cure for diabetes, once explained what it is about medical research that intrigued him so. "It's not just the gratification of knowing one is helping people," he confided, "although that probably is a more heroic and selfless motivation. Those feelings may enter in, but truly, what I find best is the feeling of going toe to toe with nature, of trying to solve the most difficult puzzles ever devised. The answers are there somewhere, those keys that will solve the puzzle and make the patient well. But how will those keys be found?"

Since the dawn of civilization, nothing has so puzzled people—and often frightened them, as well—as the onset of illness in a body or mind that had seemed healthy before. A seizure, the inability of a heart to pump, the sudden deterioration of muscle tone in a small child—being unable to reverse such conditions or even to understand why they occur was unspeakably frustrating to healers. Even before there were names for such conditions, even before they were understood at all, each was a reminder of how complex the human body was, and how vulnerable.

While our grappling with understanding diseases has been frustrating at times, it has also provided some of humankind's most heroic accomplishments. Alexander Fleming's accidental discovery in 1928 of a mold that could be turned into penicillin has resulted in the saving of untold millions of lives. The isolation of the enzyme insulin has reversed what was once a death sentence for anyone with diabetes. There have been great strides in combating conditions for which there is not yet a cure, too. Medicines can help AIDS patients live longer, diagnostic tools such as mammography and ultrasounds can help doctors find tumors while they are treatable, and laser surgery techniques have made the most intricate, minute operations routine.

This "toe-to-toe" competition with diseases and disorders is even more remarkable when seen in a historical continuum. An astonishing amount of progress has been made in a very short time. Just two hundred years ago, the existence of germs as a cause of some diseases was unknown. In fact, it was less than 150 years ago that a British surgeon named Joseph Lister had difficulty persuading his fellow doctors that washing their hands before delivering a baby might increase the chances of a healthy delivery (especially if they had just attended to a diseased patient)!

Each book in Lucent's Diseases and Disorders series explores a disease or disorder and the knowledge that has been accumulated (or discarded) by doctors through the years. Each book also examines the tools used for pinpointing a diagnosis, as well as the various means that are used to treat or cure a disease. Finally, new ideas are presented—techniques or medicines that may be on the horizon.

Frustration and disappointment are still part of medicine, for not every disease or condition can be cured or prevented. But the limitations of knowledge are being pushed outward constantly; the "most difficult puzzles ever devised" are finding challengers every day.

INTRODUCTION

A Relentless Scourge

On January 12, 2010, the small island nation of Haiti in the Caribbean Sea was rocked by a magnitude 7.0 earthquake that devastated the desperately poor country. Even before the disaster, more than 80 percent of the nation's population lived in poverty, earning less than two dollars per day. In the capital of Port-au-Prince, many lived in slum conditions—mostly in tightly packed, poorly built shacks or concrete buildings. Only half the population had access to any kind of health services, clean water, or sanitation. The earthquake made all that worse. It killed more than two hundred thousand people, collapsed or damaged more than a quarter million homes, and left up to 1.7 million people homeless.

Aid workers from around the world rushed to the nation to try to help lessen the suffering. They dug in the rubble for survivors, set up temporary hospitals for the wounded, and provided emergency shelters so the homeless would have clean water and food. Despite their efforts, ten months later more than 1 million people were still in temporary encampments. Even more lacked money to buy basic necessities. One homeless woman said, "We don't have anything, not even one dollar, because we don't have jobs."[1]

In October 2010 the difficulties were complicated by a cholera epidemic. Cholera is an illness caused by a bacterium that infects humans, making them ill. An epidemic is a condition in which an infectious disease strikes large numbers of people in a certain locale. The Haitian epidemic began in rural areas north of Port-au-Prince, where hundreds of people began experiencing severe vomiting and watery diarrhea. Within hours, the main regional hospital was flooded with patients, who crowded the parking lot and lay on the ground, begging for help. Some were dying. Humanitarian worker David Darg described the situation as a horror scene: "The courtyard was lined with patients hooked up to intravenous drips [liquid dripped into a vein over time through a tube and needle]. It had just rained and there were people lying on the ground on soggy sheets, half-soaked with feces."[2]

Mistaken Beliefs About Cholera

Because there are few cases of cholera in developed countries like the United States, many people may have mistaken beliefs about the disease. The following are a few statements that are false:

Belief: Cholera can be passed by shaking hands.

Fact: Cholera germs must be swallowed to cause infection.

Belief: Face masks can prevent the spread of cholera.

Fact: Cholera is not spread through the air.

Belief: Cholera is carried by flies, mice, and rats.

Fact: Vermin carry other diseases, but not cholera.

Belief: Water coming from a tap is safe from cholera.

Fact: Tap water may contain cholera if water sources are not disinfected.

Belief: It is safe to eat sushi, raw fish, and shellfish.

Fact: Raw or improperly cooked fish is a common source of cholera.

Belief: Everyone who gets cholera dies.

Fact: With prompt treatment, victims have a good chance of recovery.

Again, aid workers from around the world hurried to help, but by 2012 the disease had sickened over half a million Haitians, killed seven thousand, and become widespread in the country. It had spread to Haiti's neighbor, the Dominican Republic. To make matters worse, experts determined that the original strain of bacteria was evolving into two different types. That meant that the disease would become much harder to get rid of because people who had already gotten sick and recovered could fall victim to the new strain.

Recurring Pandemics

The Haitian epidemic is part of the seventh recorded pandemic of cholera to occur. A pandemic is a series of epidemics of a disease that occur throughout a large region or even throughout the world. "A pandemic is basically a global epidemic—an epidemic that spreads to more than one continent,"[3] says Dan Epstein, a spokesperson for the Pan American Health Organization, a regional office of the World Health Organization (WHO).

The first pandemic of cholera began in 1817 and lasted until 1823. In 1829 a second one broke out and lasted until 1851. Since then there have been repeated pandemics: the third from 1852 through 1860; the fourth 1863 through 1879; the fifth 1881 through 1896; and the sixth 1899 through 1923. During the course of these outbreaks, every continent but Antarctica has been hit by the scourge (disease). Millions have died, and millions more have fallen ill.

The current pandemic—the seventh—started in Indonesia in 1961. Breaking out in countries where large numbers of people were poor, living in overcrowded conditions, and uninformed about proper sanitation, the disease reached Bangladesh in 1963, India in 1964, and the former Soviet Union in 1966. In 1970 it reached sub-Saharan Africa, where it has remained entrenched for decades. For instance, Kenya has had cholera outbreaks almost every year, with the highest numbers of infections in the early 1980s, late 1990s, and 2008 to 2009. Zimbabwe experienced large epidemics in 1999, 2002, and 2008, with

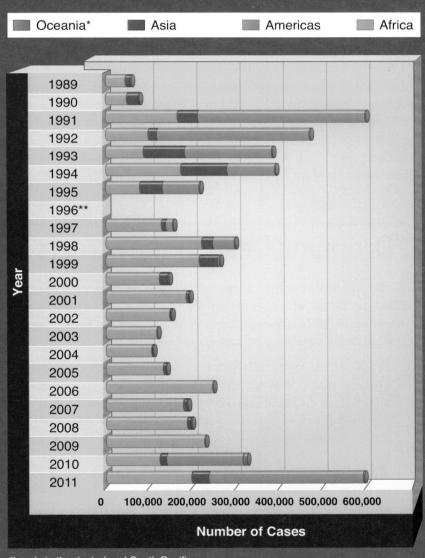

Cholera Cases Reported to WHO by Year and by Continent 1989–2011

Oceania*   Asia   Americas   Africa

Year

1989
1990
1991
1992
1993
1994
1995
1996**
1997
1998
1999
2000
2001
2002
2003
2004
2005
2006
2007
2008
2009
2010
2011

0   100,000   200,000   300,000   400,000   500,000   600,000

Number of Cases

*Lands in the central and South Pacific.
**Insufficient data.

Taken from: World Health Organization. www.who.int/gho/epidemic_diseases/cholera/en/index.html.

the latter still ongoing. Mozambique, Cameroon, and Somalia are other African countries that have also suffered outbreaks. "Where ever there is human misery you will find cholera," says Mark Pietroni, medical director of the International Centre for Diarrhoeal Disease Research, Bangladesh (ICDDR,B) in Dhaka, Bangladesh. "It thrives on malnutrition, overcrowding, and poor hygiene."[4]

North, South, and Central America remained relatively free of cholera for almost a century, but in early 1991 cases were reported in coastal areas of Peru. From there illness spread. In Central and South America, hundreds of thousands fell ill, and thousands died. No one knows exactly how the disease reached the South American continent, but it was believed to have been brought to Peru by way of infected bilgewater in a

"Dropping Dead in the Streets"

As the cholera epidemic broke out in Haiti in 2010, photojournalist Ben Depp, who lives in that country, went out to assess the situation. In the following interview with a member of the Image, Deconstructed website, he reports on what he saw:

> I expected to see people dropping dead in the streets, and, literally, that's what we found. First, we came across one victim dead on a sidewalk. Fifteen or twenty minutes down the road we came across a young man who was still alive, but barely. His mother was trying to take him to a cholera treatment center and he had collapsed a mere few hundred feet from the entrance. . . . My friend and I tried to get the staff at the treatment center to bring over a stretcher. We thought they were on their way with the stretcher, so we went back to him. . . . He died within a few minutes.

Ben Depp. "Spotlight on Ben Depp." Image, Deconstructed, 2010. http://imagede constructed.com/post/spotlight-on-ben-depp.

cargo ship, just as it was often transported from port to port in previous centuries.

In earlier outbreaks, however, no one understood what the disease was or where it came from. To them it was a terrible and mysterious enemy that killed quickly and painfully. All anyone could do was watch helplessly as victims died. A British colonel stationed in India in 1781 expressed the despair of many as he watched his men fall ill: "Death raged in the camp with horror not to be described, and all expected to be devoured by the pestilence [epidemic disease]. I attributed it to a poison, but at length found that there had been a pestilential disorder raging in the parts through which our first marches lay. . . . Our camp was already drinking the air of death and destruction."[5]

CHAPTER ONE

Cholera in Early Times

Cholera has been around for centuries, but experts disagree about exactly when it first appeared. This is because the main symptoms of cholera—diarrhea and vomiting—are also present with many other illnesses and diseases that were prevalent during ancient times. These included dysentery, typhus, food poisoning, and viral infections. No one had the modern scientific tools to see the microorganisms that caused such diseases until after the microscope was perfected in the 1600s. No one even knew that these microorganisms caused disease until the late 1800s. Because of these early limitations in identifying the disease, no one can prove that the cholera bacterium existed and caused disease before those times.

Before the bacterium was identified, there were many theories about what cholera was, why it occurred, and what people needed to do to cure it. The number of deaths from cholera continued to rise over the centuries because most of the explanations and "cures" were wrong or ineffective in fighting the disease. In fact, all they seemed to do was create fear and skepticism, as an 1854 editorial in London's *Punch* magazine illustrates. "If the doctors who write to the papers would agree in their prescriptions for cholera," the editorial states, "the public might feel grateful for the trouble taken, but when one medical man's 'infallible medicine' is another man's 'deadly poison,' . . . we are puzzled and alarmed at the risk we run in following the doctors' contradictory directions."[6]

Deadly Threat

Many historians date the beginnings of cholera to around 1817, when the first known pandemic began, but there is evidence that cholera or something with symptoms very similar to cholera existed much earlier than that. In the fourth century B.C., Greek physician Hippocrates saw many cases of a disorder he actually named "cholera." He chose the name because the Greek word *chole* meant "yellow bile," evidence that he probably noted a distinctive pale appearance of the patients' diarrhea. Hippocrates's accounts correspond to symptoms associated with

Greek physician Hippocrates used the term *cholera* in the fourth century B.C. to describe an illness with symptoms that included uncontrollable vomiting and diarrhea.

cholera today. For instance, he wrote, "At Athens a man was seized with cholera. He vomited, and was purged [had diarrhea] and was in pain, and neither the vomiting or the purging could be stopped. . . . His eyes were dark and hollow, and spasms from the stomach held him."[7] Writings in Sanskrit (an ancient language of India) dating back to 450 B.C. also reveal a lethal illness called *visuchika*, which involved diarrhea and killed its victims.

In 1543 an epidemic of what appeared to be cholera struck Goa, India. The death rate was so high that it was difficult to keep up with the burial of the corpses. Portuguese physician Garcia de Orta, who lived in India, became the first modern European to describe the disease. He also performed the first recorded autopsy on a victim of cholera. Portuguese historian Gaspar Correa also gave a vivid description of the disease at the time. The terrible suffering that he described was undoubtedly more frightening because no one knew a way to alleviate it. Correa wrote: "So grievous was the throe [struggle], and of so bad a sort, that the very worst kind of poison seemed to take effect, as proved by vomiting . . . and cramps that fixed in the sinews of the joints and of the flat of the foot, with pain so extreme that the sufferer seemed at the point of death; the eyes dimmed to sense, and the nails of the hands and feet black and arched."[8]

Other epidemics were recorded in India in the late 1700s. In 1781, for instance, a government dispatch to the directors of the East India Company, which carried on trade in the East Indies, stated:

> The disease to which we allude [cholera] has not been confined to the county of Ganjam [on the central eastern coast of India]; it afterwards found its way to this place (Calcutta) [306 miles north]; and after chiefly affecting the native inhabitants, so as to occasion a great mortality [death rate] in the period of a fortnight [fourteen days], it is now generally abated, and pursuing its course to the northward.[9]

In April 1783 cholera struck Haridwar, a city in northern India, killing twenty thousand, and caused one Indian general to write, "The loss sustained by the army in consequence of cholera morbus [deadly cholera] is very great."[10]

The First Pandemic

Virtually all early cholera outbreaks were confined to India, but around 1817 a new, more virulent form of cholera—probably a genetic mutation of an earlier form of the disease—appeared. Again, it started in India, but this time it spread more widely than earlier strains.

The outbreak began during a Hindu pilgrimage, Kumbh Mela, when worshippers traveled to the town of Jessore on the upper Ganges River. The Ganges was sacred to the worshippers because it is considered holy. The act of bathing in it or drinking it was thought to be purifying—Hindu pilgrims believed that it cleansed them of their sins and gave them heavenly blessings. If believers died, their bodies were often placed in the river. The river, which was also used for bathing, drinking, urination, and defecation, became contaminated with all kinds of bacteria because of these practices. Because people did not know about the existence of the cholera bacteria yet, they did not take precautions against spreading it. Therefore, as the pilgrims returned to their homes, they carried the infection with them, contaminating other water supplies and infecting others as they went.

By March 1820 the disease was identified in Thailand. In May of that year there were cases of it in Manila in the Philippine Islands, and in the spring of 1821 it reached China and the Middle East. In 1822 it could be found in Japan, Iraq, and Syria, and in 1823 it was reported in southern Russia and Africa. Records were not kept of the deaths, but cholera experts suggest that millions likely fell victim.

Cholera in Europe

This first cholera pandemic ended when cases of infection decreased around 1824. No one knows why they waned, but it soon became apparent that the disease had not disappeared for good. A second pandemic began in 1829, and this time it lasted twenty years. Again, cases first appeared around the Ganges River, but infection spread readily along trade routes, perhaps carried and passed in the stagnant bilgewater that collected and was pumped out of lower compartments of ships when they reached various ports.

People in Rome, Italy, tend to the dead bodies of victims of a cholera pandemic that spread through Europe around 1830.

People did not know at this time that cholera was carried in water. They felt convinced that it was somehow passed from person to person, and most blamed sailors returning from far-off places for bringing the infection to Europe and England around 1830. It struck terror there because its onset was sudden and deadly. In 1832 the German poet Heinrich Heine described it as "a masked executioner who passed through Paris with an invisible *guillotine ambulante* [traveling guillotine],"[11] because it killed people so swiftly. American physician George B. Wood observed that it seemed unstoppable: "No barriers are sufficient to obstruct its progress. It crosses mountains, deserts, and oceans. Opposing winds do not check it."[12] It soon became known as cholera morbus, Asiatic cholera, or blue death because patients' skin would turn grayish blue from dehydration before they died.

Again, keeping track of the number of victims and deaths during this wave of illness was impossible because most of those who fell ill were poor. They did not go to doctors or hospitals, and thus did not have their cases recorded. William Sproat was an exception, however. He is remembered because his was the first confirmed case of cholera in England.

Cholera Strikes England

Sproat was a dockworker living in the town of Sunderland. On October 19, 1829, after drinking water from a nearby river, he began vomiting and experiencing violent diarrhea. The family doctor could do nothing, but Sproat's wife remembered James Butler Kell, an army surgeon, who lived nearby. Kell had served in the East before moving to England and, while he did not know the cause of the disease, he had seen cases of cholera and recognized the symptoms.

Cholera Camp

Rudyard Kipling was an English poet and author, well known for his children's stories and tales of British soldiers in India in the late 1800s. The following two stanzas taken from his poem "Cholera Camp" convey the dark mood that was likely present among those who watched their mates fall ill and die during one of the many cholera epidemics that struck India.

> We've got the cholerer in camp—it's worse than forty fights;
>
> We're dyin' in the wilderness the same as Isrulites.
>
> It's before us, and be'ind us, an' we cannot get away.
>
> An' the doctor's just reported we've ten more [deaths] to-day!
>
> Since August, when it started, it's been stickin' to our tail,
>
> Though they've 'ad us out by marches a' they've 'ad us back by rail;
>
> But it runs as fast as troop trains, and we cannot get away;
>
> An' the sick-list to the Colonel makes it ten more to-day.

Rudyard Kipling. "Cholera Camp." Poetry Lovers' Page, 1896. www.poetrylovers page.com/poets/kipling/cholera_camp.html.

Kell visited Sproat and saw his sunken eyes and cold, pale hands. He felt his weak pulse and made his diagnosis. Sproat had cholera. After days of suffering, the man was seriously dehydrated. He was weak, and his fingers and legs were a dusky blue color. There was nothing Kell could do to help him, and Sproat fell into a coma and died shortly thereafter.

Because not even experts like Kell knew what was necessary to treat the disease or prevent its transmission, cholera in England did not end with Sproat's death. Sproat's son and granddaughter were soon sick, and other cases cropped up in Sunderland and then around the country. By 1832 more than fifty-five thousand people had died of cholera in England. In 1848 and 1849 the disease claimed fifty-two thousand lives. Between September 1848 and August 1849, almost seventy-five hundred people died of cholera in London alone.

A bill posted by the London Central Board of Health in 1832 alerts citizens to the symptoms and treatment of cholera. By that year, the disease had claimed more than fifty-five thousand lives in England.

CHOLERA DISTRICTS.

LOOSENESS of the BOWELS is the Beginning of CHOLERA.

Thousands of Lives may be saved by attending in Time to this Complaint, which should on no account be *neglected* by either Young or Old, in Places where the Disease prevails.

When CRAMPS IN THE LEGS, ARMS, or BELLY are felt, with LOOSENESS or SICKNESS AT STOMACH, when Medical Assistance is not at hand, *Three Tea-spoonsfull* of MUSTARD POWDER *in Half a Pint of warm Water*, or the same Quantity of warm Water with as much COMMON SALT as it will melt, should be taken as a Vomit; and after the Stomach has been cleared out with more warm Water, TWENTY-FIVE DROPS OF LAUDANUM should be taken in a small Glass of any agreeable Drink.

HEATED PLATES or PLATTERS to be applied to the BELLY and PIT of the STOMACH.

As Persons run considerable Risk of being infected by visiting those suffering from this Disease in crowded Rooms, it is most earnestly recommended that only such a Number of Persons as are sufficient to take care of the Sick be admitted into the Room.

Central Board of Health,
Council Office, Whitehall, 15th Feb. 1832.

W. MACLEAN, *Sec'.*

Cholera Reaches the New World

The Atlantic and Pacific Oceans provided a natural barrier to cholera, but the disease nevertheless arrived in North America during the second pandemic. On May 31, 1832, a ship carrying immigrants from England landed in Quebec, Canada. Many of the immigrants were ill with cholera and stayed on the ship, but those who were well enough went ashore. Seven days later, on June 6, a case of cholera was reported in the city of Montreal, 140 miles (225km) south of Quebec. Within the next few weeks, twenty-two hundred people died in Quebec, eighteen hundred died in Montreal, and the infection had been carried down the Saint Lawrence River into New York State.

The first reported New York City victim of cholera was an Irish immigrant named Fitzgerald. He and his family lived in the Five Points area of New York—an overcrowded, dirty, and disease-ridden slum in lower Manhattan. Fitzgerald survived his infection, but his family, who fell ill several days later, did not. In the crowded confines of Five Points, cholera spread quickly. American doctors did not know how to fight the disease any better than their European counterparts, and soon others in New York City were sick and dying. By the end of the summer, more than one hundred deaths a day were being reported. A letter from one young woman, written to her brother and sister on July 18, 1832, describes the scene:

> The sickness of the city is rapidly increasing. . . . It is, indeed, a very solemn spectacle to see sick persons carried through the streets in such vast numbers. Also to see 7 and 8 and sometimes 9 coffins thrown into the poor house hearse at one time to be buried. . . . Great fear and much excitement prevail almost amidst all classes of people. The cholera! The cholera! Is the common and almost the only topic of conversation.[13]

By the end of the year, most major cities in the Eastern and Midwestern United States, including Detroit, Michigan; Boston, Massachusetts; and Chicago, Illiniois, had reported

An illustration depicts a man in a horse-drawn wagon fleeing cholera after the disease was brought to North America by immigrants from England in 1832.

cholera outbreaks. New Orleans, Louisiana, where the disease raged with particular fierceness, recorded five thousand deaths in less than two months in the fall of 1832. The epidemic continued in 1833 and 1834, with the death toll for the United States and Canada rising into the hundreds of thousands.

Dealing with the Dead

Cholera was transported across the United States, too, as pioneers moved west and as thousands of men flocked to California when gold was discovered there in 1849. Some of the gold seekers followed the California trail, but others traveled by ship. They landed in San Francisco and from there often made their way by riverboat to Sacramento, in the heart of gold country. In October 1850 a passenger disembarked from the riverboat *New World* in Sacramento and collapsed and died of cholera on the wharf. The death marked the beginning of an epidemic. Within four weeks one thousand people—one-seventh of the entire population of Sacramento—had died. Many residents fled for their lives. A Sacramento reporter wrote on November 4, 1850:

"This city presents an aspect which is truly terrible. Three of the largest gambling halls are closed. The streets are deserted, and frequented only by the hearse. . . . Many deaths are concealed, and many others are not reported."[14]

Dealing with the dead was always a serious problem during epidemics no matter where an epidemic occurred. Coffin makers could not keep up with orders, so bodies lay rotting in gutters. There was no room in cemeteries, so the dead were often laid at the gates in heaps. Often, long, shallow trenches were dug, and multiple bodies were dumped in and hastily covered over. Historian George W. Ranck wrote of conditions in Lexington, Kentucky, during an 1833 epidemic there: "Many of the victims were consigned to [placed in] trunks and boxes, or wrapped in the bedclothes upon which they had just expired [died], placed in carts, and hurried off for burial without a prayer being said and no attendant but the driver."[15]

Timeworn headstones mark the graves of cholera victims from the nineteenth century at a cemetery in Wales. The bodies of those who died from cholera were often buried deep into the ground far away from inhabited areas in hopes of containing the illness.

Because of the fear of catching the disease, bodies were sometimes doused in coal tar or pitch before they were placed in graves. In England, Ireland, Wales, and the United States, cholera cemeteries were created in fields away from inhabited areas. There hundreds of nameless poor were placed deep in the ground. The areas were then avoided for years for fear that the illness would resurface.

Imbalance of the Humors

One of the most terrifying things about cholera during early pandemics was that no one knew what caused it. Many theories existed, created by those who tried to make sense of the disease. One of the oldest was postulated by the prominent Greek physician and philosopher Galen, who lived in the Roman Empire from about A.D. 130 to 201. Galen believed that the body was controlled by four humors—body fluids that influenced health and temperament—and that cholera was the result of an imbalance of those humors. (Ancient Indian medicine held similar beliefs, but thought that there were three humors.) The four humors were blood, phlegm, yellow bile, and black bile, and when they were in balance, a person was healthy. An imbalance of the four resulted in ill health, disease, or insanity.

Therapy was aimed at restoring the balance of the humors. This was done by treating symptoms, often with the use of herbs and foods associated with a particular humor. For instance, if a person had a fever and was sweating, he or she was considered to have too much yellow bile, which was believed to be hot and wet. To restore balance, dry, bland foods—associated with the opposite humor, black bile—were given.

Bloodletting was another popular therapy that was used to treat symptoms. In bloodletting, doctors made a small slit in a blood vessel in the patient's arm and allowed some blood to drain out in an attempt to drain away the imbalanced humor. The more severe the symptoms, the more blood would be drained.

An illustration shows the four humors that were once believed to control the human body. An imbalance in the humors was thought to be the cause of illness, and treatments were prescribed to counter that imbalance.

"All Smell Is Disease"

While many people believed that cholera could be explained by the humorism theory, others were convinced that it and other sicknesses arose from deadly vapors that were generated by decaying organic matter. This was the miasma theory, which also existed from the times of Hippocrates. Anything that had a bad odor—garbage, dead bodies, excrement (human waste), or any other kind of pollution—was believed to give off a poisonous miasma or gas that caused illness. In 1846 London's sanitary commissioner Edward Chadwick expressed this point of view well when he testified to parliament, "All smell is disease."[16]

Those who believed in the miasma theory were always trying different things they hoped would protect them from getting sick. For instance, many believed that wearing a soft woven fabric called flannel would ward off illness. A flannel band wrapped around the abdomen was thought to keep it warm and dry and filter miasmas that might enter the skin. The French magazine *Le Figaro* proclaimed in the mid-nineteenth century, "Today, Venus would wear a flannel girdle."[17] Heine added, "The King, too, now wears a belly-band of the best bourgeois [middle-class] flannel."[18] Another popular preventative was a waxy substance with a strong, aromatic odor known as camphor. Its vapors were supposed to counteract noxious smells. Still another was garlic; people wore it around their necks and smothered their food with it. They also carried sweet-smelling flowers or pomander balls made of perfumes or spices. Neighborhood-wide, people burned tar, pitch, sugar, or vinegar, or sprinkled chloride of lime in the home and on the streets—in the words of author Steven Shapin, "its bleachy smell giving olfactory [the nose] assurance that the miasmas had been effectively countered."[19]

Punishment from God

In combination with humors and miasmas, many people tried to explain cholera as being a punishment from God for sins, particularly the sins of immorality, drunkenness, laziness, and dirtiness. They pointed to the poor—who lived in reeking, ramshackle neighborhoods, struggled with alcoholism, and generally were struck harder by disease—as proof of their theory. As historian Charles E. Rosenberg wrote, "Cholera was a scourge not of mankind but of the sinner. . . . Most Americans did not doubt that cholera was a divine imposition [punishment]."[20]

To find relief or prevent divine punishment, many communities recommended prayer and fasting. In London on March 21, 1832, a National Day of Fasting and Prayer was called because the government was convinced that "the disease . . . was proof of the judgment of God among us."[21] In April 1833, after the disease had abated, the government again proclaimed a day of praise and thanksgiving to acknowledge "His great Goodness and Mercy in removing from us that grievous Disease with which several places in this Kingdom have been lately visited."[22]

In 1832 in America, eleven governors proclaimed days of fasting and prayer to protect their states from cholera. They also urged President Andrew Jackson to call for a national day of prayer, but Jackson refused, believing the move would violate the separation of church and state. When Zachary Taylor became president in 1849, he did not hesitate to call for a national day of prayer, fasting, and humiliation to try to counteract the disease.

Quarantine

Once people became sick, there were numerous remedies that doctors used to try to heal them. One of the remedies, castor oil, caused diarrhea and vomiting, which was believed to get rid of the poison in the body. The laxative calomel did the same, but it loosened teeth, caused hair to fall out, and destroyed the patient's intestines. There were also patent medicines such as Rymer's Peruvian Tonic Drops and Asiatic Antipestilential Essence that were tried. Most were made almost entirely of brandy or some other alcohol and did nothing to help cure patients.

The only step that actually helped to control cholera in early times was that of quarantine—forced isolation of those who were falling ill or might fall ill. When outbreaks occurred, governments passed quarantine acts so that health officers could stop people from traveling in and out of an infected area. The quarantines often included ships that arrived carrying those who were sick. Only when everyone aboard was again healthy would the vessel be allowed to depart.

Quarantines effectively stopped the disease from being spread when they were strictly enforced. But healthy people often rebelled at the thought that they were trapped inside a quarantine area and could not escape to safety. After the Russian government used quarantine and anti-travel measures in 1830–1831, mobs of peasants began rioting and attacked police, landowners, and local government officials. While the poor took to the streets, the well-to-do turned to bribery. Members of the upper class bribed officials to let them move to their country houses outside of town. Shipowners, who lost money every day their goods lay in port, paid port authorities to let them set sail before quarantines were lifted.

Despite such challenges, quarantines effectively limited the spread of cholera and other contagious diseases. For instance, when a ship from Liverpool, England, arrived in New York Har-

Cholera in the form of the Grim Reaper is depicted at the head of a British ship. The ship is met on the shores of the United States by efforts to combat it in an illustration from 1883. People arriving on ships from overseas were often subject to quarantine in an effort to contain the spread of cholera.

Quarantine Island

Swinburne Island in New York Harbor was created between 1866 and 1870 to be a quarantine station for immigrants coming to the United States. The description of it, written in 1892 by Frank Linstow White, focused on its modernity and ignored the fact that it was undoubtedly a scene of much misery and death.

> Swinburne Island, as it now stands, . . . with its rows of hospital wards—is as satisfactory as the plans intended it to be. . . . Swinburne is a hospital pure and simple and is intended solely for yellow fever and cholera cases. It has been used for this purpose ever since its completion in 1870. . . . The ten white hospital wards, opening off from both sides of a central hallway, are airy and pleasant, each ward forming a building by itself. These, as also [hospital superintendent] John Butler's dwelling, are of wood, the other buildings being of brick. Those of the patients who die are cremated, unless their relatives or friends object. The effects of the sick are fumigated with sulphur, and in case of the owner's death, if not claimed by the heirs within two months, they are delivered over to the public administrator.

Frank Linstow White. "Barriers Against Invisible Foes." *Frank Leslie's Popular Monthly*, January–June 1892. http://freepages.genealogy.rootsweb.ancestry .com/~quarantine/history4C.htm.

bor in 1866 carrying passengers with cholera, the city's health officers ordered a swift quarantine, and deaths in the city were limited to about six hundred. Eventually, Swinburne and Hoffman Islands were set up as quarantine stations in New York Harbor to prevent incoming immigrants from bringing disease into the United States.

The resistance to quarantine and the widespread fear of cholera and its deadly effects hindered but did not stop the medical community from trying to make sense of the disease and find a cure. With repeated pandemics sweeping the globe, it was clear that something needed to be done. Beginning around the time of the third pandemic, an English doctor named John Snow took the first steps by tracking a cholera outbreak to its source, thus leading the way for others to identify the bacteria and eventually control the disease.

CHAPTER TWO

Detecting Cholera

All pandemics of cholera were devastating, but the third was the most deadly. Lasting from only 1852 to 1860, it started in India then quickly spread, causing more than 1 million deaths in Russia alone. It also caused hundreds of thousands of deaths in Asia, the Middle East, Europe, and North America.

In the United States, New Orleans, Louisiana, and New York City were hardest hit. Throughout the country, most of the deaths occurred in poor communities made up of immigrants and blacks, both of whom lived in filthy, cramped conditions. Sometimes the well-to-do were also affected, however. One of the most notable was Mary Abigail Fillmore, the beautiful twenty-two-year-old daughter of former president Millard Fillmore. Abby, as she was called, had served as White House hostess from 1850 to 1853, astonishing visitors with her poise and sophistication. She seemed destined for greatness. While on a trip to her grandparents in New York State in July 1854, however, she contracted cholera. She died twelve hours after falling ill, on July 26, before her father could rush to her side.

The disease reached Britain in 1853. By the end of 1854 twenty-three thousand people had died, with the epidemic taking over ten thousand lives in London, England, alone. However, it was also in Britain and nearby Europe during this time that medical experts began focusing on the unsanitary living conditions that seemed to play a role in cholera epidemics. Scientific advancements and plenty of opportunity to observe

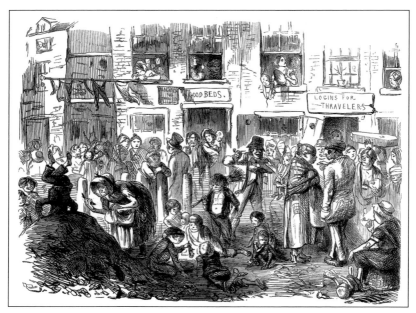

A cartoon from 1852 depicts the crowded and unsanitary living conditions that were thought to contribute to the spread of cholera in the slums of London.

the disease in urban slums helped a few key individuals identify the disease, setting the stage for prevention and treatment plans that followed in later years. John Snow took the first step—identifying where cholera lurked and how it was passed, paving the way for new studies in disease transmission. Author David Vachon writes, "For his persistent efforts to determine how cholera was spread and for the statistical mapping methods he initiated, John Snow is widely considered to be the father of epidemiology [the study of epidemics]."[23]

Crowded and Disease Ridden

The third pandemic was so deadly because living conditions had changed in the eighteenth century, bringing people closer together, which made it easier for diseases to spread within populations. Much of this change was due to the Industrial Revolution. The Industrial Revolution was the period between 1750 and 1850 in which developments in agriculture, manufacturing, mining, transportation, and technology had a powerful effect on the social, economic, and cultural conditions of the times. People flocked from the country to cities in search of jobs in textile factories, iron and coal industries, and other businesses.

By the 1800s cities were growing at an enormous rate, but because newcomers had little money, they generally made do with the poorest of housing. Large families lived in one or two rooms, packed together in huge slum neighborhoods where doors opened into filthy alleyways that were always dark and smelly. English author Charles Dickens described one such

A cartoon from the 1860s depicts a worker holding a shovel of filth near a carriage of New York City officials and a skeleton representing cholera. The accumulation of garbage and waste in the streets of large cities in the United States and Europe created conditions that led to the spread of disease.

Notable Cholera Deaths

Cholera has claimed many notable people over the decades. Some of them include:

Grand Duke Constantine Pavlovich of Russia—died 1831.

Prussian soldier and renowned German military theorist Carl von Clausewitz—died 1831.

Georg Wilhelm Friedrich Hegel, considered one of the representatives of German idealism—died 1831.

King Charles X of France—died 1836.

Former U.S. president James K. Polk—died 1849.

Mary Abigail Fillmore, daughter of former U.S. president Millard Fillmore—died 1854.

Judge Daniel Stanton Bacon, father-in-law of George Armstrong Custer—died 1866.

Russian composer Peter Ilyich Tchaikovsky—died 1893. Tchaikovsky's mother died of cholera, and his father became sick with cholera but made a full recovery.

Elliott Frost, son of American poet Robert Frost—died 1900.

neighborhood that he visited on a trip to New York in 1841: "What place is this, to which the squalid street conducts us? A kind of square of leprous houses, some of which are attainable only by crazy wooden stairs without [outside]. What lies beyond this tottering flight of steps, that creak beneath our tread?—a miserable room, lighted by one dim candle, and destitute of all comfort."[24]

Large cities like New York, London, Paris, and others all had neighborhoods like this, where conditions were right for all kinds of disease. Not only was garbage simply thrown out windows or swept into piles in the street until the trash collector arrived to pick it up, but human and animal waste was everywhere. Flies, rats, mice, and other disease-carrying vermin swarmed inside and out.

"We Live in Muck and Filthe"

In the worst neighborhoods toilets were hard to find. Whole buildings shared an outdoor latrine, known as a gully-hole, which was no more than a hole in the ground overflowing with human excrement. Those who objected to using such a foul place simply relieved themselves in convenient gutters or alleys, or used chamber pots in their rooms and dumped them out their windows. In a letter to the *London Times* in 1849, a group of poor individuals wrote: "We live in muck and filthe. We aint got no priviz [toilets], no dust bins, no drains, no watersplies [supplies]. . . . The Stenche of a Gully-hole is disgustin. We all of us suffer, and numbers are ill, and if the Colera comes Lord help us."[25]

In better neighborhoods newly developed flush toilets drained into cesspools—covered holes in the ground lined with bricks. London had about two hundred thousand of them by 1850. Ideally, the structures were watertight, and periodically the waste was dug out and carted away by night-soil men. (*Night-soil* was a polite term for human excrement.) However, cesspools were generally not emptied or well maintained, and waste regularly built up, leaked, and/or overflowed.

Most of the filth in the streets eventually drained into sewer systems, which were outdated and incapable of handling the refuse from the ever-growing population. Such systems were sometimes nothing more than open ditches, and even the best ones dumped waste into a nearby river, which could also be a source of water for drinking and washing. English investigative journalist Henry Mayhew described an open sewer ditch in London in 1849:

> In the bright light it appeared the color of strong green tea, and positively looked as solid as black marble in the shadow—indeed it was more like watery mud than muddy water; and yet we were assured this was the only

water the wretched inhabitants had to drink. As we gazed in horror at it, we saw drains and sewers emptying their filthy contents into it; we saw a whole tier of doorless privies in the open road, common to men and women, built over it; we heard bucket after bucket of filth splash into it. . . . We asked if they *really did* drink the water? The answer was, "They were obliged to drink the ditch."[26]

A cartoon from the late 1840s mocks the unsanitary state of the water supply in London during a recurrence of cholera in the city.

"WATER! WATER! EVERYWHERE;
AND NOT A DROP TO DRINK."

Coleridge.

The Infection of Baby Frances

Given these conditions, it was no wonder that when cholera broke out in the Broad Street area of London in 1854, contaminated water played a significant role in who fell ill and who did not. In this case, however, contamination was not as obvious as it was with the open sewer ditches. Thomas and Sarah Lewis lived in a crowded house on Broad Street in the Soho neighborhood of London in 1854. They did not drink from a ditch. They were fortunate enough to get their water from a community pump that had a reputation for producing some of the best-tasting, cleanest-looking water in the area.

In March 1854 Sarah gave birth to a little girl named Frances. At the time, there were cases of cholera in the city, but nothing of epidemic proportions. Nevertheless, on August 28 Frances became sick with diarrhea and vomiting. Sarah naturally changed her diapers, washed them, and tossed the filthy water into the family cesspool that lay in front of the house.

The Lewises also called the doctor, but nothing could be done to save little Frances. She died several days later. The death itself was not noteworthy—thousands of babies died in London in the 1850s—but the cause of it was. Although no one was aware of it at the time, Frances's infection marked the beginning of a neighborhood cholera outbreak that would kill hundreds.

Before Frances died her father and a neighbor upstairs fell ill. Over the next few days, more than 120 people living on or near Broad Street were dead. The London newspaper *Observer* of September 3, 1854, reported, "In Broad-street . . . when the hearses came round to remove the dead, the coffins were so numerous that they were put on top of the hearses as well as the inside. Such a spectacle has not been witnessed in London since the time of the plague."[27]

John Snow

The cholera outbreak in Soho would have been no different from many others had it not been for John Snow, who lived in London in the 1850s. Snow was one of the best doctors in the

John Snow's investigations into London's cholera epidemic in the late 1840s led to the discovery that the disease was transmitted by contaminated water.

country, perhaps the world. He was admitted as a member of the prestigious Royal College of Surgeons of England in 1838, graduated from the University of London in 1844, and was admitted to the Royal College of Physicians in 1850. Snow was also an excellent anesthetist, a physician who administers gas to cause unconsciousness during medical procedures. In 1853 he was called to attend Queen Victoria at the first chloroform-assisted royal birth.

Snow's first passion, however, was cholera—he was determined to find the cause of the disease in order to save lives. Part doctor, part detective, he began his work during the outbreak of 1848–1849, and while caring for his patients, he gathered information that might help solve the problem. From his study of chloroform and other gases, he knew that they were only effective over very short distances. So if miasmas were poisonous gases, it was unlikely that they arose from a source—say a pile of garbage—and spread through an entire neighborhood to cause disease.

Snow also knew that people who were constantly exposed to noxious miasmas should have been more likely to get sick and die than anyone else in the city. Yet his statistics showed that the night-soil men who cleaned out the cesspools and the "mudlarks" who searched the stinking mud on the banks of the River Thames for wood, metal, rope, and coal from passing ships were no more likely to fall ill than anyone else. Taking both pieces of evidence into consideration, Snow rejected the popular theory that cholera was a miasma.

Neither Miasma nor Contagion

Snow next began consideration of a new theory that was gaining in popularity—the contagionist theory. The contagionists believed that sickness could only be passed from person to person by physical contact. There was plenty of evidence to support such a theory—diseases such as smallpox, the plague, whooping cough, diphtheria, and others were common at the time and seemed to be passed from one sick individual to someone else who came in contact with him or her. The same seemed to apply to cholera most of the time. Snow wrote in 1849:

> An examination of the history of that malady [cholera], from its first appearance, or at least recognition, in India in 1817, has convinced [me] . . . that it is propagated by human intercourse [contact]. . . . The very numerous

instances, both in this country and abroad, in which cholera dates its commencement in a town or village previously free from it to the arrival and illness of a person coming from a place in which the disease was prevalent, seem to leave no room for doubting its communicability.[28]

There was a problem with the contagionist theory, though. Snow knew that cholera sometimes seemed to appear out of the blue—without there having been another case nearby. So the origin of an outbreak was sometimes a mystery. And those people who took care of cholera patients did not always get sick. So just being around and touching a person with cholera did not guarantee infection. Snow began to suspect that there was some other way the disease was passed.

As he continued his investigations, searching through medical journals and government reports, Snow came to see that there was indeed another possibility. Cholera might be linked to the city's water supplies. He began checking to see where cholera victims in two South London neighborhoods got their water. He was able to prove that those families who drank water provided by the Southwark and Vauxhall Water Company got cholera in greater numbers than those who drank water provided by the Lambeth Water Company. Southwark got its water from the Thames River after it passed through central London and had been contaminated by the city's sewage. Lambeth got its water from above the city, where the water was less contaminated. Snow was convinced that water was the key to the puzzle and stated, "[This is] very strong evidence of the powerful influence which the drinking water containing the sewage of a town exerts on the spread of cholera when that disease is present."[29]

The Broad Street Pump

While Snow was researching the London water companies, he learned of the new cholera outbreak in the Soho area. He hurried to the neighborhood to examine the water supplies. There were several public pumps set on street corners for everyone in the surrounding area to use. If he could prove that all people who fell ill got their water from one or two water sources, he would be one step closer to proving his theories.

To do that, however, he needed more information. So he turned to another physician and medical registrar, William Farr. Farr's job was to collect statistics—data regarding births, deaths, marriages, illnesses, and such—and then make sense of them in publications such as his *Weekly Returns of Births and Deaths*. Snow visited Farr and got a complete list of the names and addresses of those who had fallen ill of cholera in the Soho neighborhood. Then he began to map out the locations of the neighborhood pumps and the cases of cholera that had occurred. He eventually created a map on which he plotted each pump and each house that had cholera cases and the number of family members in each house who had fallen ill. It soon became clear that most cases were around the Broad Street pump. Then Snow began checking with those who had not fallen ill. For various reasons, they had not drunk from the pump. Snow wrote:

> I found that nearly all the deaths had taken place within a short distance of the [Broad Street] pump. There were only ten deaths in houses situated decidedly nearer to another street-pump. . . . With regard to the deaths occurring in the locality belonging to the pump, there were 61 instances in which I was informed that the deceased persons used to drink the pump water from Broad Street, either constantly or occasionally.[30]

Snow noted that in most of the cases that occurred near another pump, families had gone to the Broad Street pump for water, preferring it to nearer pumps. There were also three cases where the dead were children from other neighborhoods who went to school near the pump on Broad Street. He went on to say, "The result of the inquiry, then, is, that there has been no particular outbreak or prevalence of cholera in this part of London except among the persons who were in the habit of drinking the water of the above-mentioned pump well."[31]

Wrapping Up the Case

Next Snow decided he needed to know how cholera had gotten into the water supplied by the Broad Street pump. He turned

DEATH'S DISPENSARY.

OPEN TO THE POOR, GRATIS, BY PERMISSION OF THE PARISH.

A cartoon from 1866 depicts the Grim Reaper pumping water from a contaminated pump to unsuspecting adults and children in London. John Snow's research tied cholera deaths to a specific water pump in London.

for help to another amateur medical detective, minister Henry Whitehead, who had originally believed in miasmas and divine punishment. Determined to disprove Snow's water theory, Whitehead had gone from house to house in Soho asking endless questions. He had been won over to Snow's way of thinking, however, after he learned that some of the cleanest homes had had multiple deaths and that many of the dead were innocent widows and small children.

In his investigations Whitehead also realized that the victims had the Broad Street pump in common. But why, he asked himself, was the water from that pump "poisonous" when he had known it to be pure in the past. He finally tracked down the Lewis family as the first case of cholera in the neighborhood and learned how baby Frances's diapers had contaminated the cesspool.

Whitehead suspected that the cesspool may have leaked, so he had it dug out and found that the bricks that lined it were crumbling away. It had indeed leaked, and waste had seeped into the water that went to the pump, contaminating it with something that was causing illness. When Whitehead shared his discovery with Snow, Snow predicted, "The time will arrive when great outbreaks of cholera will be things of the past; and it is the knowledge of the way in which the disease is propagated [spread] which will cause them to disappear."[32]

The Importance of Public Health

Snow did not know that he was dealing with a bacterium when he made his discovery. However, he knew that something in the water was making people sick, and he persuaded authorities to remove the handle on the Broad Street pump. When that happened, cases of cholera in the neighborhood waned.

Evidence that the Broad Street pump was linked to the cholera outbreak, combined with the Great Stink—a time in the summer of 1858 when the smell of human waste was very strong in central London—began to motivate the leaders in countries like England and the United States to address issues of public health. Public health is the science and practice of protecting and improving the health of a community. As experts in the late 1800s began to realize that other epidemic illnesses such as typhoid and dysentery were linked to unsanitary living conditions, laws in cities like London, New York, and Paris were passed that established boards of health and recommended that drainage, water supplies, and health hazards be addressed. This included building safer sewer systems, collecting and disposing of garbage in remote landfills, and providing clean water.

Wherever such improvements were made, cholera epidemics virtually disappeared. The fifth pandemic (1881–1896) was the last to affect Europe, and the last serious outbreak in the United States was in 1910–1911, when the steamship *Moltke* brought infected people from Naples, Italy, to New York City. Vigilant health authorities isolated the infected on Swinburne Island. Only eleven people died in that outbreak, including a health-care worker.

The Great Stink

The Great Stink was a time in the summer of 1858 during which the smell of untreated sewage became unbearable for people in central London. The smell was a result of a combination of factors. First, the Thames River, which ran through the city, was heavily polluted with runoff from the innumerable cesspools that Londoners used daily. It was also befouled by waste from factories, slaughterhouses, and other pollution-producing businesses that used it as a city dump. Second, that summer was unusually warm and humid, encouraging the growth of bacteria that led to the stench of decay.

By June the resulting smell was so overwhelming that well-to-do Londoners fled the city. Members of the House of Commons hung curtains soaked in chloride of lime to try to damp down the smell. After two weeks heavy rains came, the weather cooled, and the immediate crisis ended. Parliament, however, rapidly authorized the funds necessary for famed engineer Joseph Bazalgette to build a massive sewer system so the Great Stink would not be repeated. Bazalgette's sewers not only helped cleanse the Thames, they helped end cholera epidemics in the city and became a model for sewer systems in New York City and other cities across the western United States.

Germs, Not Miasmas

At the same time that city leaders were improving water and sanitation systems, researchers were continuing their investigation of microorganisms—tiny living organisms that cannot be seen by the naked eye. The interest in them had been ongoing for decades, ever since Dutch scientist Antoni van Leeuwenhoek had seen yeast cells, blood cells, and single-celled moving organisms, which he called animalcules, under his microscope in the 1670s. Building on Leeuwenhoek's work, physician Nicolas Andry argued in 1700 that some of the microorganisms he saw, which he called worms, were responsible for most of the diseases that attack mankind. Other researchers, like German zoologist and microscopist Christian Ehrenberg (1795–1876), continued the study of these tiny microorganisms, which were eventually divided into categories that included bacteria, algae, fungi, and protozoa.

Although bacteria had been discovered by the mid-1800s, there were still many believers in the miasma theory. However, in the 1860s French physician Louis Pasteur dealt the theory a blow when he disproved the theory of spontaneous generation—that something such as a disease could arise from inanimate matter. He did this by conducting an experiment. He boiled broth so that any organisms living in it would be killed, then put it in vessels that contained filters to keep out particles such as bacteria in the air. As time passed, nothing grew in the broth. After the vessels were opened and exposed to the air, however, living organisms grew in the broth. Pasteur concluded that the living organisms came from outside the jars, rather than being created in the broth. Pasteur's work gave support to a new theory that was gaining in popularity—the germ theory, the belief that infectious disease was a result of living microorganisms.

The germ theory was definitively proved in 1890 by German physician and researcher Robert Koch when he took the bacterium that he believed caused anthrax, grew it in his lab, and then infected animals with it, causing new cases of anthrax. Koch had already been credited with identifying the rod-shaped bacterium that caused cholera in 1883. The bacterium had been isolated by Italian anatomist Filippo Pacini in 1854, but Pacini's work had been ignored due to widespread support

German physician Robert Koch's discovery of the cholera bacteria in 1890 led to widespread acceptance that the disease was caused by an organism that was spread from person to person.

for the miasma theory. Koch's discovery built on Pasteur's work and findings, however, and after it was published, the fact that cholera was caused by an organism that was passed from person to person in contaminated water was accepted both by the public and by the scientific community.

It took many more years before the cholera bacterium was fully analyzed, its structure scrutinized, and its method of attack determined. Today, more is known about this deadly disease than ever before. And, as journalist Tina Rosenberg writes, "Cholera should not be a terror."[33] Despite these advances, however, cholera remains a terror, in large part because understanding the disease is only the first step in controlling and eradicating it.

CHAPTER THREE

What Is Cholera?

There were important discoveries concerning cholera made during the time of the third pandemic, but no one came close to stamping out the disease. Therefore, fourth, fifth, and sixth pandemics followed earlier ones. Despite the repeated epidemics, which caused millions of deaths, there were few additional breakthrough discoveries about cholera until the twentieth century. With the illness confined largely to the poorer classes, scientists and medical experts focused on understanding and eradicating more common diseases such as diphtheria, smallpox, tuberculosis, and polio. Not until the late 1900s did physicians and researchers like John Mekalanos, Rita R. Colwell, and others do more to answer the question "What is cholera?" At that time they began to add significantly to the medical community's knowledge of the bacterium, including its genetic makeup, where it thrives, how it attacks the human body, and who is most at risk of infection.

Vibrio Cholerae

The bacterium that Robert Koch saw under his microscope in 1883 is today called *Vibrio cholerae*, or *V. cholerae*, a one-celled organism that is only 0.3 microns in diameter and 1.3 microns in length. (A micron is one-thousandth of a millimeter.) Vibrio bacteria are a group of bacteria that have a curved rod shape and a flagellum—a long, whip-like tail that helps them move. They are called vibrio because when Filippo Pacini first saw them under his microscope in 1854, they appeared to vibrate. *V. cholerae* is also covered with fine, hair-like structures called pili that are used to establish contact with cells in the human body.

V. cholerae is part of a group known as Gram-negative bacteria. Gram staining was invented by Hans Christian Gram around 1884 in order to be able to see bacteria more easily under a microscope. The cell walls of Gram-positive bacteria retain a violet color when washed with a crystal violet stain, while the walls of Gram-negative bacteria do not. About 90 percent of Gram-negative bacteria cause disease because of a layer in their cell walls that contains toxins. Other examples of Gram-negative bacteria are *Bordetella pertussis*, which causes whooping cough; *Salmonella typhimurium*, which causes food poisoning; and *Yersinia pestis*, which causes bubonic plague.

A colored scanning electron micrograph of *Vibrio cholerae* bacteria shows the organism's curved rod shape and long whip-like tail.

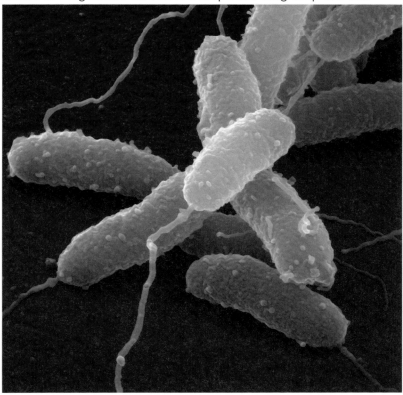

The genetic makeup of *V. cholerae* has been known since 2000. The bacterium has 3,885 genes, which are carried on two circular chromosomes. Genes are made up of deoxyribonucleic acid (DNA) and are the basic units of heredity that determine all the characteristics of an organism. Chromosomes are thread-like strands that carry the genes. In *V. cholerae*, one chromosomal ring is about three times larger than the other. The larger ring carries genes that allow the bacterium to replicate, produce proteins, maintain its cell wall, and cause disease. Researchers have also been able to determine that the gene for toxicity that is present in *V. cholerae* was originally part of a bacteriophage—a virus that infects bacteria. So at some time in the past, *V. cholerae* blended that outside genetic material into its own chromosomes.

Different Strains of Cholera

Cholera bacteria mutate easily, creating different strains or serogroups. Mutation is the permanent change in the makeup of a gene that results in changes in the cells of an organism. It can occur as the result of exposure to radiation, viruses, chemicals, or from errors that occur when cells divide. Depending on which gene mutates, changes can be produced in everything from the appearance of an organism to the way it reacts to its surroundings. In the case of *V. cholerae*, mutations create differences in toxicity that make certain types or serogroups extremely dangerous to humans.

DNA, or gene, profiling is used to distinguish between serogroups of *V. cholerae*. The process was first conceived in 1984 by British geneticist Alec Jeffreys at the University of Leicester in England and uses variations in the genetic makeup of living organisms to make identifications. With *V. cholerae*, a sample of genetic DNA from bacteria in one outbreak is analyzed so that the structural makeup of every gene is understood; then that profile is compared to the genetic makeup of bacteria from another outbreak. If the genetic makeup is the same, the profiles of the two strains are the same and they are believed to come from the same source. If not, researchers are looking at two different serogroups coming from two different sources.

As of 2012 there were over 150 known cholera serogroups worldwide. Most serogroups cause very mild symptoms in humans, but two—serogroups 01 and 0139—can be deadly. Serogroup 01 is broken down into two biotypes (strains or groups of organisms with the same genetic makeup)—classic and El Tor. Pandemics four, five, and six were caused by the classic biotype, and it is likely that earlier pandemics were, as well. El Tor, identified in 1905, has been largely responsible for the seventh pandemic. Serogroup 0139, which was identified in 1996, is similar in genetic structure to El Tor. So is a new El Tor hybrid strain that appeared in Bangladesh in 2009, but both these latter strains are much more deadly than the original El Tor. Physician Amit Ghosh at the National Institute of Cholera and Enteric Diseases in Kolkata (formerly Calcutta), India, says, "The dehydration caused by cholera is extremely severe when infected with the El Tor hybrid and hence mortality rates are higher."[34]

Getting information about strains is important so that public health officials can respond as quickly as possible to outbreaks. For instance, analysis of the cholera bacteria in the Haitian outbreak of 2010 determined that it was a strain that

El Tor

The strain of *V. cholerae* known as El Tor was first identified in 1905 at a quarantine camp on the Sinai Peninsula in El-Tor, Egypt, by a German physician, Felix Gotschlich. Bacteria found in the feces of six pilgrims returning from Mecca reacted with anti-cholera serum, which proved that the bacteria were cholera. El Tor was identified again in an outbreak in 1937, but the pandemic caused by the strain did not arise until 1961.

When it comes to symptoms, an El Tor infection is relatively mild compared to the classical strain of cholera. Patients may not express symptoms for a week. This characteristic, however, allows carriers to infect a greater number of people.

A member of the United Nations peacekeeping force in Haiti takes a sample of waste near an infected river system as part of an effort to identify the strain of cholera responsible for an outbreak in the region in October 2010.

was previously found in Southern Asia. Nepalese troops who had entered the country as part of the United Nations (UN) earthquake relief effort were from that area, and cholera is endemic (occurs regularly) in Nepal. They were stationed at a camp in Haiti where sanitation facilities were inadequate. Their untreated waste could have flowed into the Artibonite River, where cholera bacteria were found. The outbreak also began shortly after the Nepalese troops arrived.

The troops were checked and found not to be infectious. The Haitian government sponsored an investigation into the source of the infection, which they could not link positively to the Nepalese camp. However, some experts—such as French epidemiologist Renaud Piarroux, who led the investigation—still suspected that the Nepalese troops were to blame. Piarroux stated, "It [the outbreak] started in the centre of the country, not by the sea, nor in the refugee camps. The epidemic can't be of local origin. That's to say, it was imported."[35]

Cholera in the Environment

When cholera outbreaks occur, experts always look for contamination in water sources, because water is the home of the
bacterium in the environment. *V. cholerae* is found worldwide
in both marine and freshwater habitats, although it grows
best in the warm, slightly salty waters of river mouths, bays,
or other shallow coastal areas. Some areas where cholera is
always naturally present are the Bay of Bengal, the waters
off the west coast of South America, and the Gulf of Mexico.
Director of the National Science Foundation Rita R. Colwell,
who studies cholera in the environment, says, "We have come
a long way to the integrative point of view that *Vibrio cholerae*,
the causative organism of the disease cholera, is a normal
component of the ecosystem—an organism that can never be
eradicated but only controlled."[36]

For many years scientists believed that *V. cholerae* could
not live more than a few hours outside the human body. In
the 1980s, however, researchers discovered that, as part of
the bacterium's life cycle, it can live for months if not years
attached to the hard exoskeleton of tiny crustaceans called
copepods, which feed on algae. In this way it also travels as
the crustaceans follow their food source, moving with the tides
and covering fairly long distances.

When conditions are too cool or not salty enough, the
bacterium can also lie dormant in water for long periods of
time. Under such conditions, it changes from a rod shape to a
smaller, round shape. It forms colonies and secretes a protec-
tive covering called a biofilm that is wrinkly and resistant to
chlorine. (Chlorine normally kills *V. cholerae*). In this stage it
does not grow and is not toxic, but when conditions change
and nutrients are reintroduced, it can then change back into a
rod-shaped infectious organism.

Most infectious periods occur during warm, wet seasons,
when algae bloom and copepods are plentiful. For instance,
more cases occur during the April-to-June rainy season in
Haiti and the June-to-October monsoon season in Bangladesh.
Increased numbers of cholera cases have also been tracked
to occurrences of El Niño, a periodic warming of the surface

Cholera Life Cycle

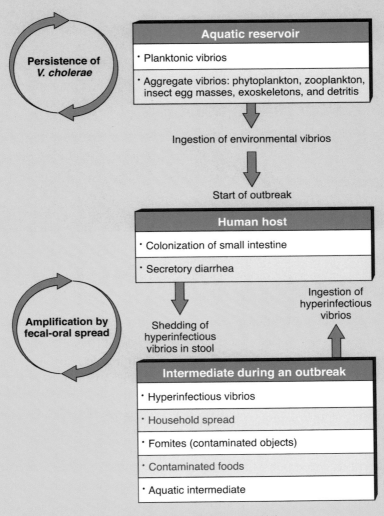

Persistence of V. cholerae

Aquatic reservoir
- Planktonic vibrios
- Aggregate vibrios: phytoplankton, zooplankton, insect egg masses, exoskeletons, and detritis

Ingestion of environmental vibrios

Start of outbreak

Human host
- Colonization of small intestine
- Secretory diarrhea

Amplification by fecal-oral spread

Shedding of hyperinfectious vibrios in stool

Ingestion of hyperinfectious vibrios

Intermediate during an outbreak
- Hyperinfectious vibrios
- Household spread
- Fomites (contaminated objects)
- Contaminated foods
- Aquatic intermediate

Taken from: Nature Reviews/Microbiology. www.MHSHhd.wikispaces.com/cholera.

water of the Pacific Ocean that causes unusual global weather patterns. Colwell believes that global warming will contribute to more cholera in the future. She says, "With carbon dioxide increasing in the atmosphere, global warming and more rainfall, river flow could increase, lowering salinity and driving up *V. cholerae* populations."[37]

A woman drinks from a pump surrounded by floodwater in Bangladesh. People can become infected with cholera by drinking contaminated water or eating food that has been cleaned or prepared with contaminated water.

Route of Infection

Humans become infected by *V. cholerae* only if they ingest (take into their mouths) water or food contaminated with the microbes. The bacterium is not passed through the air or by brushing up against an infected person. Physician Cory Couillard emphasizes, "In many countries it is common for individuals to think that it is transmittable from one person to another. This is untrue; cholera cannot be transmitted through casual contact with an infected person. Cholera will commonly spread rapidly due to shared meals and water that is contaminated."[38]

More than 1 million cholera bacteria are needed to cause illness. This is because most, when ingested, do not survive the acidic conditions of the human stomach. In large quantities, however, enough survive to be passed to the small intestine, where the environment is much less acidic. There they are able to thrive and, by the use of their flagella, push through the mucus layer that lines the walls of the small and large intestine. When they reach the wall, they attach themselves, then begin to grow and reproduce explosively. Victims can excrete 500 million cholera bacteria in every teaspoon (5mL) of feces.

Once attached to the intestine, cholera bacteria begin to secrete a potent toxin called choleragen. It is this toxin that causes illness. It activates an enzyme in the intestinal cells that converts the cells into pumps that extract fluids from blood and tissues. The fluid floods the intestine as diarrhea and carries away important electrolytes such as sodium, potassium, chloride, and bicarbonate that the body needs to function.

Stages of the Disease

When people become infected with a toxic strain of cholera, they commonly go through four stages of the disease. The first is the incubation period, which can last anywhere from two hours to five days. This is the time when the bacteria are passing through the stomach to the intestine and attaching themselves to the intestinal wall. Victims usually feel no symptoms during this stage.

The second stage of infection is called evacuation or full development. This lasts from three to five days and is characterized by full-blown symptoms that come on suddenly. The most characteristic are copious amounts of diarrhea and vomiting. A person can lose gallons of fluids and electrolytes within a

Confusing Terms

Vibrio cholerae has only been found in two animal populations other than humans—shellfish and plankton. There are animal diseases that are called cholera, but none are related to human cholera. The terminology can be confusing.

Avian cholera is caused by the Gram-negative bacteria *Pasteurella multocida* and causes diarrhea and death in turkeys, chickens, ducks, geese, canaries, and raptors. As in human cholera, infected birds often die within six to twelve hours. Swine cholera, also known as swine fever, is caused by a virus termed classical swine fever virus. Symptoms include fever, skin lesions, and seizures, and death often quickly follows.

day or two—and all these fluids contain millions of dangerous cholera bacteria. Diarrhea has a characteristic milky look and is often referred to as "rice-water" stool because it contains flecks of mucus and cells from the lining of the intestine.

The full-development stage is not only frightening and painful, but humiliating as well. Ivy Kuperberg, who volunteered in one of Haiti's cholera tent hospitals in 2011, recalled:

> As a medical student, I learned about cholera and how the profusely watery diarrhea and vomit is a result of an enterotoxin produced by the cholera bacteria. . . . What the literature does not describe, however, is how it feels to watch a 65-year-old woman vomit a waterfall of bile-green water for the fifth time in a day. . . . She had been there with her grown daughter who not only emptied the bucket when it was full, but then also cleaned her mother after each session of diarrhea in full view of the five other patients who shared her room. By the fourth day, my last day in the camp, her condition was finally improving. But, I was still heartbroken that she had spent so many days in such a miserable and degrading position.[39]

An elderly woman with symptoms of cholera is pushed in a wheelbarrow to a hospital in Harare, Zimbabwe, during an epidemic in 2009. Without care, people with cholera can become dehydrated quickly, which can lead to death.

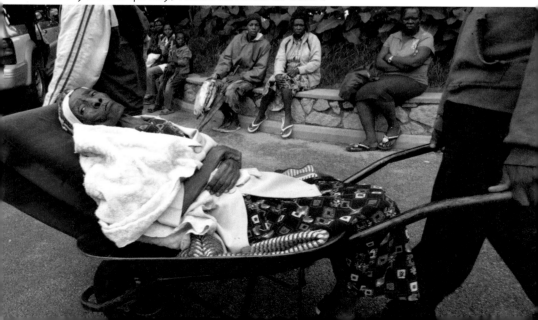

If untreated, patients become dehydrated and can quickly pass to the third stage, which is collapse. Outward signs of dehydration include weakness, irritability, sunken eyes, extreme thirst, and dry, shriveled skin. The loss of sodium, chloride, and potassium produces an electrolyte imbalance, which causes muscle cramps. The loss of fluids results in a drop in blood volume and blood pressure. The heartbeat becomes weak and irregular. Hands and feet become cold and clammy, and because of a lack of oxygen in the blood, they turn a dusky blue color. Kidney failure may follow, so that the body is no longer able to filter impurities from the body. No urine is passed, poisonous wastes build up, and the patient slips into a coma. Persian physician Muhammad ibn Zakariya Razi was describing a patient in A.D. 900, but his words are still appropriate for the collapse stage today: "The pulse fails, and the breathing is attenuated [weakened]; the face and nose become thin; the color of the skin of the face is changed, and the countenance of the dead succeeds. The extremities become cold and there is cold perspiration, and there are spasms of the hands, feet, and legs. There is urgent thirst, which cannot be satisfied."[40]

The fourth stage of the disease—death—usually follows very shortly. A patient may linger for several days, but often, it is only two to three hours between onset and death. Sometimes patients collapse and die before they can reach a treatment center. "It's shocking to see somebody die of dehydration," says physician Vanessa Rouzier, who works with cholera patients in Haiti. "I saw a young 20-year-old collapse in front of me from paralysis because he had lost too much potassium. A healthy, strapping 20-year-old! This is unheard of!"[41]

Those who recover from an attack of cholera gain some immunity to the disease, but the amount of immunity is not definitely known, and reinfection is possible. Immunity is a condition in which the body resists a disease through antibodies produced in response to exposure to the disease. Cholera antibodies are large proteins that are capable of identifying and neutralizing cholera bacteria. Immunity from cholera, if it occurs, rarely lasts more than a year.

Those at Risk

Persons at greatest risk for catching cholera are those who live in areas where the bacterium is endemic. This includes parts of Africa, Asia, the Middle East, and South America. Among these, however, there are groups who are more likely to fall ill, have more serious symptoms and complications, and/or die more quickly. For instance, children—especially malnourished children—fall ill in greater numbers because they have not yet built up the same immunities that adults may have. They may also die more quickly because they dehydrate more rapidly than adults.

Those who naturally produce less stomach acid—children and the elderly—get sick more often because it takes fewer bacteria to infect them. The same is true for anyone who takes antacids, H-2 blockers, and/or acid reducers such as Prilosec, Prevacid, Aciphex, and Protonix to treat conditions such as gastroesophageal reflux disease or peptic ulcers. Studies show that when gastric acidity has been lowered, it can take only one-hundredth as many cholera bacteria to cause disease as it would in an adult with normal levels of stomach acid.

Those individuals who have HIV/AIDS or another medical condition that weakens their immune system are also more likely to catch the disease. Although they do not develop more severe cases of cholera than other patients, their recovery can take longer. Stanley Takaona, deputy president of the Zimbabwe HIV/AIDS Activist Union, says, "This disease leaves people completely wasted; it is very hard for many of our members to recover."[42]

Persons who have type O blood group are more likely to get sick and get more serious infections than persons with other blood groups. Blood is generally divided into four main groups—A, B, AB, and O, the designation stemming from inherited antigens that are found on red blood cells in the blood and other cells in the body. No one fully understands the reason for the link between type O blood and cholera infection, but those who have type O report more diarrhea, vomiting, muscles cramps, and need for hospitalization. Their outcome for recovery is also poor. At the other extreme, persons with type AB blood have the greatest resistance to the disease.

Finally, women who are pregnant are liable to have complications if they catch the disease. A baby cannot catch cholera in the mother's body, but it does not receive enough oxygen, blood flow, or necessary nutrients when the mother becomes dehydrated. The result is premature labor and/or death of the baby. Midwife Felipe Rojas Lopez, who helps treat women with cholera who are in the late stages of labor and delivery at Isaie Jeanty Hospital in Port-au-Prince, Haiti, pointed out in December 2010: "It's not unusual that we see such cases. We've done 17 deliveries. The mothers have all survived, but most of the babies had died in the womb by the time they were admitted. Of the three babies who were born alive, we had to resuscitate one. The other two were in good shape and we treated them as we would any healthy baby."[43]

A pregnant woman suffering from cholera waits for care at a hospital in Haiti during an outbreak of the disease in 2010. Pregnant women, children, the elderly, and people with weak immune systems are particularly at risk of the effects of the disease.

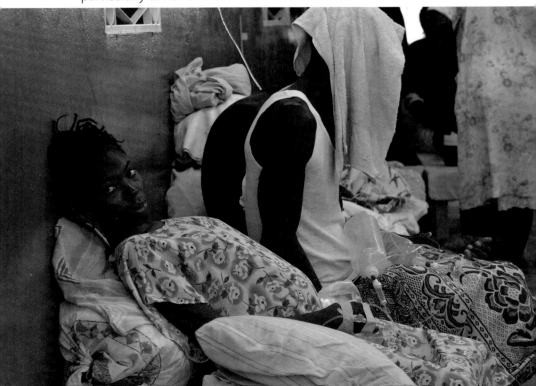

No matter whether one is in a high-risk group or not, prompt treatment is the key to surviving a case of cholera. Without treatment, the death rate can be higher than 50 percent. With treatment, it can be as low as 1 percent. Cholera expert Dhiman Barua writes, "Experience . . . has shown that while the introduction of cholera into a country cannot be prevented, its spread within the country can be checked. Treatment is so successful today that no cholera patient need die if treatment can be made available."[44]

CHAPTER FOUR

An Easily Treatable Disease

For all the terror that cholera outbreaks produce in the world today, the disease is easily treatable and, with treatment, does not usually kill its victims. Despite this, there are still an estimated 3 million to 5 million cases and 100,000 to 120,000 deaths annually due to the disease. Outbreaks of cholera still occur in developing countries, where large portions of the population do not have modern sanitary facilities, clean water, and the knowledge to avoid disease. Of the thirty-two countries that reported deaths from cholera in 2010, twenty were in Africa. There were also cases in India, Afghanistan, Nepal, Thailand, and Haiti. As cholera specialist Stephen Calderwood of Massachusetts General Hospital emphasizes, "This is not a problem of yesterday or somewhere else. It's a problem of today."[45]

While there are still too many cases and too many unnecessary deaths from cholera, health officials get some satisfaction in knowing that the death rate from cholera is lower than ever before. That is because more people are aware that treatment is available and seek it out. For instance, even though Peru was struck unexpectedly by cholera in 1991, the country had in place an extensive treatment program, an epidemic field-investigation service, and laboratory resources. In addition, people in urban areas knew to go to a hospital at the first symptom. Enrique Jacoby and Bruno Benavides of the Institute of Nutritional Investigation in Lima, Peru, explain, "What have we learnt from the experience of Peru? We believe that in cities and towns, people should be encouraged to go quickly to hospitals, since immediate seeking of appropriate treatment seems to have saved many lives."[46]

"A Common Ordeal Here"

As in earlier times, cholera still strikes in areas where water is not clean or disinfected and where sanitation systems are inadequate. Such conditions are often found in poor countries like Haiti, refugee camps like the Dadaab refugee complex in Kenya, and urban cities like Dhaka, the capital of Bangladesh. Dadaab is home to some half a million people who have fled war, famine, and food shortages in neighboring Somalia and now live in the middle of nowhere, crowded together with little hope for the future. In dry years water is chronically in short supply. Residents collect and use every drop, even if it has to be scooped out of dirty puddles or rivulets in the streets. In some parts of the camp, primitive latrines are shared by over one hundred people. They are impossible to keep clean, so excrement overflows and drains out into the open. Cholera struck the camp in 2011, believed to have been brought there by newly arrived refugees, and officials fear that more outbreaks are likely to occur.

Dhaka, a fast-growing city in one of the world's most densely populated countries, has 16 million residents. In its slums people live crowded together in shacks and make do with dilapidated sanitation systems. The city is edged by heavily polluted rivers, where cholera is a regular threat. Almost all water is pumped from deep wells, but the pumps require electricity to run. Regular power shortages allow pressure in the pipes to fall and sewage and other contaminants from the ground to leak in. Volunteer health worker Anita Ashfaqunnesa says, "Cholera is a common ordeal here."[47]

There are hundreds of refugee camps and urban slums like Dadaab and Dhaka in developing countries around the world. In almost all of them, conditions are favorable for cholera.

The skyline of Dhaka, Bangladesh, rises beyond a group of shacks that are part of that city's network of slums, where overcrowding, insufficient sanitation systems, and water pollution make cholera a constant threat.

Their residents live with substandard water and sanitation systems. Sewer pipes leak and septic tanks are not regularly emptied, with the result that their contents leach out into the ground and pollute groundwater. Some people lack any kind of sanitation facilities and must resort to practices that increase the risk of spreading cholera. One such practice is the use of so-called flying toilets—plastic bags that are filled with feces and then thrown out a window. Another is the practice of open defecation. For instance, Port-au-Prince, Haiti, resident Antonina Tanisshe reports, "We don't have no toilet at all. We do it in the sea."[48] She and others simply crouch on a cement ledge and relieve themselves over a tidal canal that edges the slum.

Diagnosing Cholera

Because the early symptoms of cholera are very similar to many other gastrointestinal diseases that plague the populations that are susceptible to cholera, diagnosis must be quick and definitive so appropriate measures can be taken. Quick diagnosis not only helps ensure proper treatment, it can allow public health officials to begin working to control the outbreak as soon as possible.

The process of confirming that a person has cholera always begins with a fecal sample from the patient. That sample can

What to Do If You Think You Have Cholera

If you return home from a locale where cholera is present and show symptoms of severe diarrhea and vomiting, go immediately to a hospital or call a national emergency telephone number such as 911 in the United States, 999 in the United Kingdom, or 112 in the European Union. If your symptoms are not severe, call a family doctor or general practitioner. Be sure to tell him or her that you suspect your illness may be cholera.

Be sure to stay well hydrated until you receive help. Drinks such as water, juice, and soda will not adequately replace lost fluids and electrolytes. Instead, use an oral rehydration solution such as Equalyte or Rehydralyte for adults or Pedialyte for children. If no oral rehydration solutions are available, make your own by combining 1 quart (1L) of bottled or boiled water with 8 level teaspoons (39mL) of table sugar and 1 level teaspoon (5mL) of table salt. Be sure that you and those around you wash your hands often with soap and water or some other disinfecting solution.

then be viewed under a microscope to see if *V. cholerae* bacteria are present. This is a relatively slow approach, however. Samples must be gathered and taken to a lab where a microscope is available. A visual exam can also be unreliable, because it can be difficult to distinguish cholera rods from coliform and other rod-shaped bacteria. Also, fewer bacteria are passed as infection progresses, so they can be more difficult to find.

A more definitive approach involves an agglutination, or clumping, test, which is also performed in a laboratory. After collecting a fecal sample, a small amount is placed in a nutrient medium of agar and broth. In this medium at room temperature, bacteria, if present, will grow and multiply. After two to four hours, a drop of *Vibrio cholerae*, or *V. cholerae*, antiserum—fluid that possesses cholera antibodies that are produced by the body to fight infection—is added and left to react. If cholera is present, clumping of the bacteria and the antibodies gives a curdled look to the suspension, which is visible to the naked eye within one hour.

Because cholera cases often occur in regions that are not close to any laboratory, in 2000 researchers at the Pasteur Institute in Paris began developing a test that could be carried out even in remote locales—the rapid cholera dipstick test. As the name suggests, a paper dipstick, pretreated with a reactive substance, is inserted in a fecal sample. After approximately ten minutes, the stick is read. If two colored lines appear, the patient has cholera. If only one line appears, the test is negative. The rapid diagnostic test detects both serogroups—O1 and O139—and is 94 to 100 percent accurate. As an institute press release stated in 2003, "They [dipstick tests] are easy to use, and require no specific technical training. . . . The simplicity and efficacy [effectiveness] of these dipsticks should improve patient care . . . even in the remotest regions."[49]

A technician at a laboratory in Cambodia holds a testing plate swabbed with a fecal sample to test for the presence of cholera bacteria. In areas without access to a laboratory, cholera can be confirmed with a simple dipstick test.

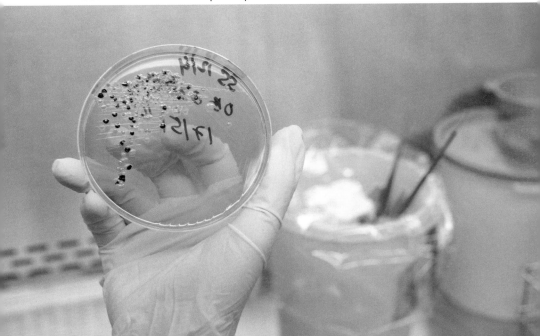

Fluids Are the Key

Even before a patient is diagnosed with cholera, treatment can begin. This is because the most effective treatment for cholera is the introduction of fluids. The official use of fluids as a treatment for cholera is fairly modern, and giving fluids to cholera patients goes against early doctors' beliefs that poison needed to be drained out of a person's system. Still, there were some early physicians who considered fluids and dared to try them. The Indian physician Sushruta wrote prescriptions for rice water, coconut milk, and carrot soup to treat diarrhea in 800 B.C. In 1831 Irish physician and researcher William Brooke O'Shaughnessy noted that the blood of cholera patients lacked much of the water and saline ingredients of healthy patients' blood. He suggested that death might be avoided if a solution of salts and warm water was injected into a patient's vein. A year later English physician Thomas Latta read O'Shaughnessy's suggestion and decided to try it. Choosing an elderly woman

A child with cholera is given fluids intravenously in order to combat the dangerous dehydration that the disease causes. The introduction of fluids administered orally or through an IV is key to treating cholera.

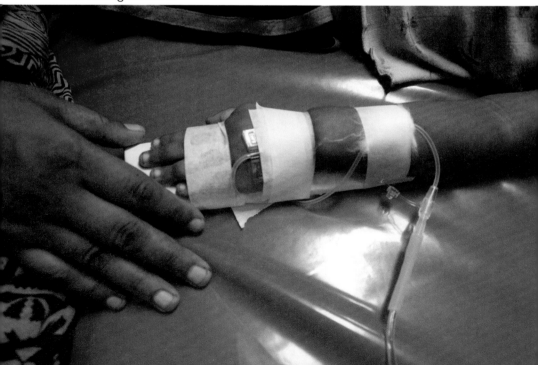

with cholera, he injected her with saline solution and watched the results. He wrote, "Ounce after ounce was injected . . . when six pints had been injected, she expressed in a firm voice that she was free from all uneasiness." Unfortunately for the patient, Latta left her in the care of another doctor who did not continue the fluids treatment, and as a result she died of the disease. Latta commented, "I have no doubt the case would have issued in complete reaction [ended in recovery], had the remedy, which already had produced such effect, been repeated."[50]

Despite Latta's success, rehydration therapy for cholera was not widely used until 1971. That year, during a cholera epidemic in Bangladesh, physician Dilip Mahalanabis at the International Centre for Diarrhoeal Disease Research, Bangladesh (ICDDR,B) instructed his staff to distribute a drinkable mixture of water, glucose (sugar), and salts that approximated the makeup of fluid being lost from the body. Over three thousand patients were treated, and results were remarkable. Most recovered; the death rate was only 3.6 percent, compared to the expected 60 percent. Mahalanabis's treatment became known as oral rehydration therapy (ORT), and in the words of physician Wiley Henry Mosley, his results helped ORT to "really hit the map . . . it probably took that kind of a demonstration in a crisis to really document what could be done."[51]

Oral Rehydration Therapy

Today, ORT is standard treatment for cholera, because it is highly effective and easy to administer, even to young patients. Journalist and public health expert Joshua N. Ruxin testifies, "I've seen infants survive the worst cholera symptoms thanks to spoonfuls of solution administered tenderly by their mothers. Remarkably, the solution is effective even when it must be mixed with dirty water."[52] Less than 1 percent of patients die if lost fluids and electrolytes are replaced. Health officials rely on the combination of glucose, sodium citrate, potassium chloride, and sodium bicarbonate mixed with water, which is administered orally or, if the patient is extremely ill, intravenously. Prepackaged mixes are available, but a solution of 8

Hospital workers in Dhaka, Bangladesh, prepare packets with a mixture of salt and sugar to be used for oral rehydration therapy in the treatment of cholera.

teaspoons (39mL) of sugar, 1 teaspoon (5mL) of salt, and 1 quart (1L) of clean water is also effective.

Treatment works best if it is begun early in infection, and massive amounts of fluid must be used. "The biggest mistake is that patients do not get enough hydration fast enough," says Mark Pietroni of the ICDDR,B. "You have to give huge amounts of IV fluid in the first three hours—seven or eight liters. In Dhaka at the end of April you see people with IVs in each arm and leg. But as soon as the patient can drink, you switch them to oral rehydration."[53]

Rehydrating patients literally brings them back from the brink of death. Those who arrive at a clinic barely showing a pulse can be sitting up and drinking just a few hours later. Their skin goes back to normal, their thirst subsides, and their pulse becomes strong. Public health specialist Jon E. Rohde remembers one case involving a rural village in Bangladesh where a man had collapsed from severe cholera. He was near death, and no oral rehydration solution was available, so Rohde was forced to make do with more basic ingredients—molasses, sea salt, and water. He recalls:

> Guessing at the correct proportions I hastily mixed up a solution in the pot and started spooning it into the man's slack cheeks. . . . Patiently persisting, I managed to get a liter or so into his stomach, and he started to come around, drinking with some new vigor. In an hour he was sitting up and departed in my jeep for the hospital some 25 kilometers away. When I arrived there in the evening, he was walking stiffly around the ward. . . . I was a convert to "simple solutions."[54]

Supplemental Treatments

While many patients only need ORT to recover from cholera, experts have found that there are some who benefit from supplemental treatments. For instance, a 2005 study in Bangladesh showed that if children were given zinc supplements, the severity of their symptoms decreased and they recovered much sooner. Zinc is now becoming a standard part of cholera therapy. According to the ICDDR,B, "Zinc is a success story, a therapy which has been able to reduce death of children suffering from diarrhoeal diseases and cholera by up to 50%."[55]

Antibiotics are also a part of therapy if cases are particularly severe. Doxycycline, azithromycin, erythromycin, tetracycline, furazolidone, and ciprofloxacin have all been successfully used along with intravenous rehydration. Mass administration of antibiotics is not recommended during cholera outbreaks, however, for fear that the bacterium will develop resistance. Resistance can occur if bacteria that have mutated or are not killed by the antibiotics quickly replicate, creating a cholera infection that does not respond to antibiotic treatment. The concern seems to be justified. In India in 2000 scientists reported the emergence of several cholera strains that did not respond to several antibiotics. The strains of cholera seen in Haiti are

Enormous Risks

The dangers of refugee camps were illustrated in 2012 when, faced with war and famine, many Somalians moved into camps around their capital city, Mogadishu. The camps are potential breeding grounds for cholera and other diseases, as Dominic Wabala writes in the *Star*, the third-largest newspaper in Kenya.

> Over 200,000 internally displaced people flocking into camps in Mogadishu are at risk of contracting water-borne diseases following the filling up of the 6,000 toilets they use daily. . . . Killian Kleinschimidt, the deputy UN humanitarian coordinator for Somalia, fears that this might contaminate the available water when the rains come. "These 6,000 latrines in Mogadishu are full and there is no site to take the stuff. The mayor does not know where to put it. . . . Something should be done about it. . . ."

> The OCHA [UN Office for the Coordination of Humanitarian Affairs] Somalia boss said the distribution of humanitarian aid in the 500 Mogadishu settlements for the IDPs [internally displaced persons] is a challenge because most of the water is heavily contaminated and has to be well treated before being used. . . . "We live in a big toilet in Mogadishu so it needs heavy treatment particularly in the rainy season. The risks in terms of hygiene are enormous."

Dominic Wabala. "Cholera Outbreak Fears in Mogadishu." *Star* (Nairobi, Kenya), May 24, 2012. www.the-star.co.ke/lifestyle/128-lifestyle/77344-cholera-outbreak-fears-in-mogadishu.

The sea buckthorn plant is among the herbal and traditional medicines that researchers are investigating to determine their possible use in the treatment of cholera.

also resistant to some antibiotics. Sujit Bhattacharya, director of the National Institute of Cholera and Enteric Diseases in Kolkata, India, says, "Our list of antimicrobial agents still effective against cholera is shrinking."[56]

Because of the danger of antibiotic resistance, researchers continue to look for other ways to treat cholera that might be useful in the future. For instance, some are studying the cystic fibrosis gene in humans, because there is evidence that persons who carry only one gene for cystic fibrosis do not catch cholera. Others are reexamining herbal and traditional medicines such as the antidiarrheal dragon's blood plant and gastrointestinal remedy sea buckthorn to see if either might be a part of treatment in the future.

Obstacles to Treatment

Although prompt and vigorous treatment can save lives and limit outbreaks, there are those who, for various reasons, do not get treatment when they are infected. For instance, some individuals become infected and show few or no symptoms of cholera. In fact, research shows that only one in ten people infected with cholera actually develop symptoms, and some of those symptoms may be mild. But although they do not feel sick, they can have bacteria in their feces for seven to fourteen days after becoming infected. Thus, they can pass the bacterium to other people without knowing it. Individuals who have a disease but show no symptoms are commonly known as carriers.

An example of the potential danger of such carriers involves a woman from the Philippines known as Cholera Dolores. In 1962 she suffered a very mild attack of cholera, was not treated with antibiotics, and seemed to recover, but at times had cholera bacteria in her feces until 1966. An investigation proved that it was the same strain of cholera that she had originally contracted. Apparently cholera bacteria had become established in her gallbladder and were being released periodically. Fortunately, Dolores and her family lived in an isolated rural area, but if she had lived in a populated region, she could have caused untold harm to those around her.

Dolores did not seek treatment because she did not know she was infected, but sometimes people avoid help even when they know they are sick. They are afraid of being shunned by family and friends, of being quarantined, or of going to the hospital. Virginie Nzouatcha, a native of Yaoundé, Cameroon, in Africa, recalls, "My neighbor died at home. He was hiding his condition, fearing he'd be quarantined. He tried self-medication but, unfortunately, he succumbed to the disease."[57]

"We Must Press for . . . Awareness"

Ignorance, suspicion, misunderstanding, and a lack of funds are other hindrances to treatment. Unnecessary cholera deaths occurred in the Papuan tribe in Indonesia in the 1960s because members of the tribe distrusted the Indonesian government after having suffered violence at the hands of the military. Thus, they hesitated to seek or accept medical treatment when the epidemic broke out, believing that the government was poisoning them.

Similarly, in March 2009 a mob in a village in Mozambique attacked and killed a Red Cross volunteer, two government

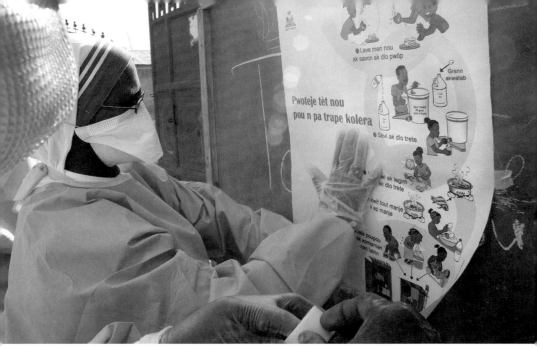

A health-care worker hangs a poster about the prevention and treatment of cholera at a clinic in Haiti as part of an effort to combat misunderstanding and ignorance about the disease.

health workers, and a police officer who were adding chlorine to the drinking water to disinfect it. The mob mistakenly believed that the workers were pouring cholera germs into their water.

In Haiti in December 2010, out-of-control mobs killed twelve voodoo priests who were suspected of spreading the disease by spells and black magic. Voodoo is a religion often associated with the practice of magic and communication by trance with ancestors and animistic deities, common in Haiti and other Caribbean islands. "The victims . . . were stoned or hacked with machetes before being burned in the streets," says communications ministry official Moise Fritz Evens. "Voodoo practitioners have nothing to do with the cholera epidemic. We must press for an awareness campaign about the disease in the communities."[58]

Knowledge and public health awareness will help those who get sick to seek help quickly, but money is vital, and a lack of it is probably the greatest obstacle to treatment. Without money, there can be no oral rehydration packets, antibiotics, and other necessities. Health-care workers will not be able to afford to care for the ill. And with thousands of cases of cholera occurring every year, the cost for treatment can run into millions of dollars.

Funding for cholera does not involve just treatment, either. The goal of health officials is not just curing the sick, but preventing future cases from occurring. Prevention involves education, upgrading sanitation facilities, and a host of other costly factors. In Haiti alone, the cost of building safe wells, piped sewage systems, septic tanks, and so on could cost more than $1 billion. Those who fight cholera therefore continue to push for better funding, just as they push for education, awareness, and improvements in public health in developing countries everywhere.

CHAPTER FIVE

Wash Hands, Boil Water

There have been many lessons learned from cholera over the years. Disease can be carried in water. People can be infectious even when they have no symptoms. Careless sanitary practices cause needless deaths. World health officials have also learned that developing countries often cannot effectively cope with cholera on their own. Therefore, governments and organizations who have the money necessary to institute the changes needed to prevent cholera try to help so that the still-deadly scourge can be controlled.

"Boil It, Cook It, Peel It or Forget It"

Preventing cholera is relatively easy for people who live in developed, industrialized countries. Laws and agencies make sure that water is disinfected, sanitation systems work, and food is safe to eat. In the United States, for instance, the U.S. Environmental Protection Agency works with water and sewage treatment operators to prevent contamination of water. The U.S. Food and Drug Administration tests imported and domestic shellfish and monitors the safety of U.S. shellfish beds through a shellfish sanitation program.

According to the World Health Organization (WHO), travelers from developed countries who visit areas where they can catch cholera have only to follow the rule "boil it, cook it, peel it or forget it"[59] to prevent infection. That means people should

Afghan workers wash carrots in a polluted river in Kabul. People in developing nations who lack access to clean water or knowledge of how the disease is spread are at particular risk for cholera.

drink and brush teeth with boiled, bottled, or chlorinated water; eat only food that is completely cooked and hot; avoid sushi and other incompletely cooked fish and seafood; and eat only fruits and vegetables such as bananas and cucumbers that can be peeled immediately before eating. It also helps to wash hands frequently in soap and water. Ignoring such guidelines has proved to be dangerous. In early 2011 nine people from the United States became sick with cholera after eating improperly cooked lobster at a wedding in the Dominican Republic.

Those living in developing countries where cholera is endemic and health standards are not high face greater challenges. They do not always know how to prevent the disease. Even if they do know, they may not be able to get what they need to prevent infection. As of 2011 at least 11 percent of the world's population—783 million people—did not have access to safe drinking water, and 2.5 billion lacked improved sanitation. Jonathan Lascher of Partners in Health, an organization that helps provide health care to the poorest people in Haiti, says, "People here know they should be washing their hands with soap. They know they should be drinking treated drinking water. They know they should be using latrines. But that's not always possible. It's . . . a question of access."[60]

Organizational Efforts

People in developing countries do not have what they need to prevent cholera because their governments are not always willing or able to give disease prevention the attention it deserves. In some cases they may be hampered by their own instability. For instance, Somalia's shaky central government struggles to control pirates who have ravaged the country since a civil war in 1991, hindering the government's ability to battle diseases such as cholera. Other countries, like the Kenyan government, may be short of money and overwhelmed with refugees who are fleeing civil war or natural disasters in neighboring countries. Tina Rosenberg gives another reason: "Governments, fearing stigma and a loss of tourism, often cover up cholera, and international organizations sometimes go along with the fiction."[61]

Because of these obstacles, in recent years government and nongovernment organizations from developed countries around the world have stepped in to help prevent and control cholera. These organizations range from the WHO—responsible for providing leadership on global health matters—to groups like Charity: Water and the Water Project, which specialize in the creation of local wells and water systems. Efforts usually involve improving water quality, sanitation facilities, and educational opportunities. Although there is sometimes a lack of coordination among groups, which can result in money being wasted and aid not reaching everyone who needs it, their work is undeniably valuable. At best, they bring much-needed expertise and a stable stream of funding to the countries.

The WHO and UNICEF—the United Nations Children's Fund—are leading organizations that actively support cholera-prevention activities. Both provide technical advice and train health professionals at regional, national, and international levels in prevention. They also focus on distributing information and guidelines on cholera and other epidemic-prone diseases to health professionals and the general public.

In 2000 UNICEF and the WHO hosted a Millennium Summit of the United Nations, which set development goals that, among other things, aim to cut in half the proportion of the population without access to safe drinking water and basic sanitation by 2015. Progress toward reaching the goals has been uneven. Some countries have already achieved their goals, while others are not on track to realize any. Musician and humanitarian Paul David Hewson, also known as Bono, observed in 2010, "We have a lot to prove, but if the M.D.G. [Millennium Development Goals] agreement had not been made in 2000, much less would have happened than has happened. Already, we've seen transformative results for millions of people."[62]

Another international agency that works to prevent cholera and other diseases is the Water Supply and Sanitation Collaborative Council, based in Geneva, Switzerland. The council provides a venue for individuals and organizations concerned with water, sanitation, and hygiene in developing countries to share ideas. It is currently involved in thirty-six countries. Its members pioneered the simple but effective notion of Water, Sanitation and Hygiene (WASH) programs, which are promoted by various groups such as UNICEF and the Centers for Disease Control and Prevention (CDC). WASH programs include practical information on things like hand washing and disposing of waste as well as instructions for identifying safe and unsafe water sources, protecting food from contamination, and preventing disease transmission from person to person. Former UN secretary general Kofi Annan says, "WASH has helped to place the issues of clean water, basic sanitation

A UNICEF worker in Guatemala demonstrates how to use chlorine tablets to prepare clean drinking water for poor and rural residents. UNICEF is one of the leading organizations in providing technology and education to prevent cholera.

and good hygiene firmly in the public consciousness and on the political agenda."[63]

Clean Water and Latrines

Clean water is one of the keys to controlling cholera, and efforts generally focus on both community and individual improvements. Because it is impossible to provide state-of-the-art water systems to every community in developing countries, disinfecting current systems using chlorine is the key. Those who work with public water systems are taught to ensure that adequate amounts of chlorine are supplied to drinking water to kill bacteria. Adequate supplies of chlorine must be kept in stock, and water supplies also need to be regularly checked to be sure that chlorination equipment is working.

At the individual level, families are also taught to use chlorine tablets to purify any water they collect and use in their homes. The cholera organism is also readily killed by heat, so boiling water purifies it, too. In India and Bangladesh, health officials teach women that a technique called sari filtration is also adequate to remove bacteria. A sari is a garment worn by Hindu women that consists of a long piece of cotton or silk wrapped around the body and draped over the head or shoulder. Women learn that folding a clean sari eight times and using it to filter drinking water effectively reduces contaminants, including cholera bacteria.

While disinfecting water is one important step in preventing cholera, the creation of efficient sanitation systems is just as important. Sewer and septic systems are the gold standard of sanitation, but in many instances, just getting people to build and use latrines is a step in the right direction. Latrines can be simple pits or trenches dug into the ground. They can also involve more sophisticated systems such as composting toilets and pour-flush systems that use a small amount of water. All must be used correctly, however, so that waste does not leak. They must be covered, cleaned regularly, and either be filled in or have the waste removed from them and properly disposed of. They must be

A nurse distributes chlorine tablets and oral rehydration salts to a woman in Bolakpur, India, in 2009 after an outbreak of cholera in the area. The use of chlorine tablets is one of several ways that water can be purified before it is used for drinking or cooking.

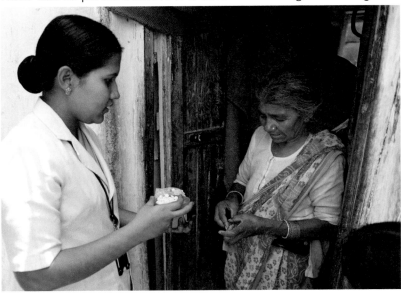

located away from living spaces and water sources. They must also be adequate for the number of people who use them.

To ensure that such standards are met, organizations such as UNICEF have also become champions of Community-Led Total Sanitation (CLTS) projects. This is a method for motivating communities to eliminate open defecation by building

"Doing the World's Dirty Work"

In 2000 independent consultant Kamal Kar pioneered the idea of Community-Led Total Sanitation. In 2010 the magazine *Foreign Policy* named him one of the Top 100 Global Thinkers and praised him "for doing the world's dirty work."

Kamal Kar spends much of his time thinking about something that many of us would rather not: where and how people poop. It's not pretty, but improving sanitation is one of the most important aspects of overcoming poverty and water-borne diseases such as typhoid and cholera. . . . That's where Kar, an agricultural scientist by training, comes in. Sanitation is about people, not pipes, he says: "It's not a question of counting toilets." Once toilets and sewers are built, getting communities to use them is often a tougher challenge: for example in his native Bangladesh, where defecating indoors had been strictly taboo. He suggests such tactics as giving children whistles to blow whenever they see someone defecating outside—a sort of constructive peer pressure.

And it works. After Bangladesh adopted Kar's ideas, latrine coverage skyrocketed from just 33 percent in 2003 to more than 70 percent today. Kar's "community-led total sanitation" method is now at work in 39 countries around the world.

Quoted in *Foreign Policy*. "The FP Top 100 Global Thinkers," December 2010. www .foreignpolicy.com/articles/2010/11/29/the_fp_top_100_global_thinkers?page=full.

latrines and using them. One of the obstacles to improving sanitation is the widespread unwillingness to talk about or acknowledge the problem of human waste. For most people, relieving themselves is a private event. Urinating or defecating in an isolated spot seems preferable to building and using a latrine that all their neighbors can see.

Educating the Community

Much of the prevention of cholera relies on chlorination of water and the appropriate deposit of human waste, but educating people is the most important way to curb the disease. Some organizations such as the Red Cross send teams into neighborhoods to teach basic practices such as hand washing before preparing food and using dippers rather than hands to scoop water or food from communal bowls and jars.

Some organizations encourage local radio stations, television stations, and newspapers to broadcast health education messages. The Pan American Health Organization, the WHO, and the Dominican Republic's government helped sponsor a National Day of Education and Prevention of Cholera on November 30, 2010. The day began with a message from the country's president that urged people to learn to prevent the disease. His message was carried on all main radio and TV stations in the nation. In addition, flyers were distributed on major streets and in parks of the capital of Santo Domingo while loudspeakers filled the air with ways to avoid infection.

Organizations also recruit community and religious leaders to lead educational campaigns and get people involved. In small villages in Africa, for instance, leaders and traditional healers can be powerful influences when it comes to introducing new practices and enforcing rules for sanitation and clean water. For instance, as part of a CLTS project in Sierra Leone, chief Boima Swarray set two-person teams to patrol the streets every morning. Villagers who practiced open defecation were taken to him for consultation and counseling. He stated, "Eighty percent were willing to adopt the project after awareness was created."[64] To further increase enthusiasm for the project, Swarray also held a village-wide hygiene festival

A Red Cross volunteer speaks to food vendors at a market in Port-au-Prince about cholera prevention after an outbreak in 2010. The Red Cross is one of several organizations providing cholera education and prevention information at the individual and community level.

where children danced and sang about what was formerly un-mentionable: "Kaka don don o, Lef for kaka na bush" (no more excreta in the open and stop defecating in the bush.)[65]

Children Promote Change

Children are excellent promoters of change in developing countries, and schools are places where teachers have the opportunity to teach cholera prevention. In the Lusaka province of Zambia, which was hit hard by cholera in 2009, for instance, UNICEF sponsored a Your Life is in Your Hands campaign. Designed to appeal to children, the campaign included cartoons and performances by a traditional drama group and a popular young Zambian entertainer. Lusaka's district commissioner, Christah Kalulu, also spoke to more than two thousand elementary school students about changing their attitudes and behavior toward health and disease prevention. "Hygiene is about you," she said. "All of you should make sure that you practice good habits of washing your hands with soap before you place your hands on food, after visiting the toilet and even after playing. You never know what germs you may have encountered."[66]

Once they have heard the message, children are encouraged to tell their parents when they get home. Hygiene promoter Farah Sylvestre, who helps educate children in Haiti, says, "It's important that children understand how to protect themselves. These children are a vehicle for carrying the cholera prevention message to adults—a means for bringing about a positive change in the behavior of older people."[67]

The efforts pay off not just in Zambia and Haiti but in other regions as well. In Nepal, for instance, sixth grader Manju

Hand Washing Made Fun

Beginning in 2008 governments around the world began taking action to promote better sanitation with an annual Global Handwashing Day, always scheduled for October 15. The day is sponsored by organizations and companies ranging from UNICEF to Procter & Gamble, and the focus is on children learning while having fun.

Games such as Get Bubbly, which teaches hand washing, are popular and available on the Global Handwashing Day website. During Get Bubbly, children try to cross a line to tag the leader, Bubbly. They can only move if they make correct motions for commands given. For instance, if Bubbly says, "Make scrambled eggs!" children must put their fingers together in the shape of a bar of soap, scrub their hands, then do the motion of stirring an egg in a pan. For the command "Use the toilet!" children must first squat down and then do the motion of picking up a bar of soap and washing their hands.

Those who fail to do all the motions or do them in the wrong order cannot advance. However, the first child to tag Bubbly and shout "clean hands" gets to be Bubbly for the next round of play.

Schoolchildren in Soweto, South Africa, wash their hands with soap as part of an event to promote hand washing as a lifesaving habit. Children are often the target of hygiene education efforts because they can, in turn, teach their parents and other members of their household what they learned.

Chaudhary of Baijalpur village recalls, "When we started out, I was quite embarrassed since . . . we didn't have a latrine at home. I argued with my parents, who are very poor and were quite hesitant in the beginning. But soon they came around when they realized how serious I was."[68]

Vaccines

While great emphasis is placed on clean water, sanitation, and community education, there are those in the health community who also want to focus on vaccines to prevent cholera epidemics. Traditionally, vaccines have not been widely used because of their imperfections, the low risk of infection in developed countries, and the prohibitively high cost for people in developing nations. The CDC does not recommend using cholera vaccines, and they have never been available in the United States. However, as time passes and conditions change, that thinking is changing, too. Physicians Matthew K. Waldon, Peter J. Hotez, and John D. Clemens observed in 2010, "Even though there is no imminent threat of cholera in the United States, we believe that our country should stockpile cholera vaccines for rapid deployment to parts of the world that suddenly find themselves at high risk for this disease. . . . The humanitarian benefits of rapid deployment of cholera vaccines to areas at high risk for major cholera outbreak . . . could be enormous."[69]

The idea of using cholera vaccines to prevent widespread outbreaks is not new. The first was developed in the late nineteenth century, when Spanish physician Jaime Ferran created a whole cell vaccine after growing cholera bacteria in his laboratory. The vaccination process consisted of three injections in the arm and produced limited immunity. Ferran was criticized—first for putting human lives at risk as he tested it, and second for trying to keep his vaccine a secret until he could market it.

Today's vaccines are better than Ferran's, but they are nowhere near perfect. Two kinds are widely available—Dukoral and Shanchol. Each requires two doses (more doses are required for children), which stimulate the immune system to produce antibodies against cholera without making a person

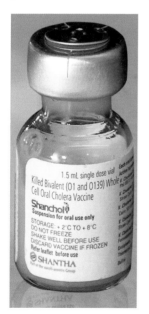

sick. The doses are delivered by injection four weeks apart, and several more weeks must then pass before persons receiving them are protected. The vaccines are not recommended for children under two years of age, and they provide protection for no more than six months. Currently, about a third of the people getting the vaccine still contract cholera.

Shanchol is one of two vaccines that are currently widely used to inoculate people against cholera.

Putting Vaccines to the Test

Despite cholera vaccine shortcomings, in April 2012 the WHO launched the Haiti Cholera Vaccine Project, hoping to reduce the numbers of cases of cholera in that country. Due to a shortage of vaccine, the program did not cover the entire country. Rather, Cite de Dieu, one of the worst slums in Port-au-Prince, was targeted. Health practitioners went door-to-door to vaccinate persons who had preregistered for the program. Nadia Simone, whose family lives next to a ditch filled with sewer-tainted water, participated because her young daughter fell ill with cholera in 2011. She says, "All my children will be vaccinated, because I don't want cholera to come back to my house."[70]

Many criticize the effort as a waste of money that they say could be better used to build water- and sewage-treatment systems. Those projects could take years, however. Lascher of Partners in Health points out that Shanchol, the vaccine his group uses, is much more affordable than Dukoral and can save lives now. He asks, "We know that there's a safe and effective oral cholera vaccine that can help prevent people from getting cholera again. Why wouldn't we do that?"[71]

There is also hope that at least one more vaccine will be available in the near future. As of mid-2012 Peru-15, or Cholera-Garde, was being tested in India but had not yet passed all of its clinical trials. Its advantages are that it could be administered in a single dose and could be given to children. To gain approval for widespread use, however, it needs to give high levels of protection for three years to those who are living where cholera is endemic. Its safety must also be established among persons who are HIV positive.

Cholera in the Future

It is clear that while much has been learned about cholera, much still remains to be discovered and much work still needs to be done before it is defeated. Better, less expensive vaccines are needed. To achieve this, researchers such as professor of biosciences Hiroshi Kiyono at the University of Tokyo are testing the possibilities of inserting genetic material from *Vibrio cholerae*, or *V. cholerae*, into plants such as rice and potatoes to create an oral vaccine that is cheap and does not have to be refrigerated, as current vaccines do. Kiyono explains:

> The part of the body that requires immunity to the cholera bacteria is the mucosa of the intestinal digestive tract. . . . The problem is that before it can reach the mucosal immune system associated with the intestine, the vaccine is usually digested or broken down. Rice is the ideal delivery system for the digestive tract, since it has a unique and stable protein storage system which can tolerate digestive enzymes in the intestine.[72]

A better understanding of cholera in the environment is also necessary to help eradicate this disease. So is a better understanding of people who do and do not fall ill from the disease. Infectious disease expert Calderwood says:

> [The Haitian outbreak] represents an opportunity to look at cholera in a different genetic background. Haitians are mostly of African descent, whereas Bangladesh is of an Asian descent. There may be quite different genes predisposing to cholera in these two different genetic backgrounds. . . . [Also] we have not studied the interaction of cholera and HIV very much, and I think HIV may have an impact on immune responses that follow cholera, and therefore immune responses that might follow a vaccination. And so the outbreak in Haiti, since HIV is more prevalent there than in Bangladesh, gives an opportunity to try to answer that question.[73]

Experts emphasize that knowledge is the key when it comes to cholera. And with modern technology, scientists and government agencies can better work together to learn about and control the disease. Eliminating it entirely, however, is still just a dream. *V. cholerae* appears to be widespread in the waters of the world. With worldwide travel becoming more commonplace, it is possible that the bacterium will show up in unexpected locales that were never threatened before. Finding funds for a global elimination campaign is unlikely. Even if developing countries have the money and the will to fight the disease, unexpected disasters such as droughts, earthquakes, and wars could undermine their best intentions.

Therefore, it is likely that cholera will be a part of life for a long time. Physician and author Gerry Greenstone points out:

> The [impact] of future outbreaks depends not so much on the organism as on human actions and the environment surrounding the organism. If there is malnutrition there will be cholera; if there is poor sanitation there will be cholera; if there is war there will be cholera. We have the knowledge and the technology to eradicate this disease, but do we have the will and the determination? If not, then cholera will remain the scourge that never dies.[74]

Notes

Introduction: A Relentless Scourge

1. Quoted in Joseph Guyler Delva. "Quake Camps at Risk as Haiti Cholera Tops 200." Reuters, October 23, 2010. http://mobile.reuters.com/article/topNews/idUSTRE69L21520101023?i=1&irpc=932.
2. Quoted in Delva. "Quake Camps at Risk as Haiti Cholera Tops 200."
3. Quoted in Martin F. Downs. "What Is a Pandemic?" WebMD, 2005. www.webmd.com/cold-and-flu/features/what-is-pandemic.
4. Quoted in Andrew Marshall. "In Bangladesh, a New Way to Fight Cholera." *Time*, February 15, 2011. www.time.com/time/world/article/0,8599,2048937,00.html.
5. Quoted in Nottidge Charles MacNamara. *A History of Asiatic Cholera*. London: Macmillan, 1876, p. 38.

Chapter One: Cholera in Early Times

6. Quoted in Steven Johnson. *The Ghost Map*. New York: Riverhead, 2006, p. 50.
7. Quoted in Dhuman Barua and William B. Greenough III, eds. *Cholera*. New York: Plenum, 1992, p. 3.
8. Quoted in MacNamara. *A History of Asiatic Cholera*, p. 33.
9. Quoted in MacNamara. *A History of Asiatic Cholera*, p. 39.
10. Quoted in MacNamara. *A History of Asiatic Cholera*, p. 39.
11. Heinrich Heine. *French Affairs: Letters from Paris*. Vol. 7. London: William Heinemann, 1893, p. 162.
12. Quoted in Robert MacNamara. "The Cholera Epidemic of 1832 Killed Thousands and Created Panic." About.com, 2012. http://history1800s.about.com/od/crimesanddisasters/a/Cholera-Epidemic-Of-1832.htm.
13. Mary S. Briggs, ed. *The Ferguson-Jayne Papers, 1826–1938*. Interlaken, NY: Heart of the Lakes, 1981. www.oneonta.edu/library/dailylife/health/1832newyorkcholera.html.

14. Quoted in Irma West. "Plagues of the Gold Rush." *Sierra Sacramento Valley Medicine*, August 2001. www.ssvms .org/ssv_medicine/archives/2001/04/articles/0104-west.pdf.

15. George W. Ranck. *History of Lexington Kentucky: Its Early Annals and Recent Progress.* Cincinnati, OH: Clarke, 1872. http://rootsweb.ancestry.com/~kyfayett/cholera1833 .htm.

16. Quoted in Johnson. *The Ghost Map*, p. 114.

17. Quoted in Steven Shapin. "Sick City." *New Yorker*, November 6, 2006. www.newyorker.com/archive/2006/11/06/0611 06crbo_books?currentPage=2.

18. Shapin. "Sick City."

19. Shapin. "Sick City."

20. Charles E. Rosenberg. *The Cholera Years: The United States in 1832, 1849, and 1866.* Chicago: University of Chicago Press, 1987, pp. 40, 43. www.stanford.edu/dept /HPS/154/May13RosenbergP1to98.pdf.

21. Quoted in Robert McR. Higgins. "The 1832 Cholera Epidemic of East London." *East London Record*, 1979. www .mernick.org.uk/thhol/1832chol.html.

22. Church of England. *A Form of Prayer and Thanksgiving to Almighty God.* London: George Eyre and Andrew Spottiswoode, April 14, 1833, p.1.

Chapter Two: Detecting Cholera

23. David Vachon. "Father of Modern Epidemiology." *Old News*, May & June 2005. www.ph.ucla.edu/epi/snow /fatherofepidemiology_part2.html#TWO.

24. Charles Dickens. *American Notes for General Circulation.* Classic Literature Library, 1843. www.charles -dickens.org/american-notes-for-general-circulation /ebook-page-49.asp.

25. Quoted in Shapin. "Sick City."

26. Quoted in Spartacus Educational. "Cholera." www.sparta cus.schoolnet.co.uk/DIScholera.htm.

27. Quoted in Johnson. *The Ghost Map*, p. 109.

28. John Snow. "On the Mode of the Communication of Cholera." John Show Archive and Research Companion. http://johnsnow.matrix.msu.edu/MCC1-PMCC-51MT.pdf.

29. Quoted in Vachon. "Father of Modern Epidemiology."

30. John Snow. "The Cholera Near Golden Square, and at Deptford." *Medical Times and Gazette,* September 23, 1854. www.ph.ucla.edu/epi/snow/choleragoldensquare.html.

31. Snow. "The Cholera Near Golden Square, and at Deptford."

32. Quoted in Johnson. *The Ghost Map,* p. 181.

33. Tina Rosenberg. "Saving Lives in a Time of Cholera." *New York Times,* April 8, 2012. http://query.nytimes.com/gst /fullpage.html?res=9C05EFDE103EF93BA35757C0A9649D 8B63&pagewanted=all.

Chapter Three: What Is Cholera?

34. Quoted in Kounteya Sinha. "Deadly Cholera Strain Hits India." *Times of India,* April 11, 2009. http://articles .timesofindia.indiatimes.com/2009-04-11/india/28031071 _1_cholera-strain-severe-dehydration-and-death-watery -diarrhoea.

35. Quoted in BBC News. "Haiti Cholera: UN Peacekeepers to Blame, Report Says." December 8, 2010. www.bbc.co .uk/news/world-latin-america-11943902.

36. Rita R. Colwell. "Cholera and the Environment: A Classic Model for Human Pathogens in the Environment." National Science Foundation, February 14, 2004. www.nsf .gov/news/speeches/colwell/rc040214aaascholera.htm.

37. Colwell. "Cholera and the Environment."

38. Cory Couillard. "Preventing Cholera Outbreaks." *Botswana Guardian,* April 20, 2012. www.botswanaguard ian.co.bw/newsdetails.php?nid=3679&cat=BG%20Style.

39. Ivy Kuperberg. "Coming Back: Ex-Volunteer and Visitor Assists in Cholera Hospital." Saint Damien Hospital, January 18, 2011. http://saintdamienhospital.nph .org/2011/01/18/coming-back-ex-volunteer-and-visitor -assists-in-cholera-hospital.

40. Quoted in Barua and Greenough. *Cholera,* p. 4.

41. Quoted in Richard Knox. "In Haiti, Bureaucratic Delays Stall Mass Cholera Vaccinations." *Shots* (blog), National Public Radio, May 27, 2012. www.npr.org/blogs/health 2012/03/27/149403215/in-haiti-bureaucratic-delays-stall -mass-cholera-vaccinations.

42. Quoted in IRIN News. "Zimbabwe: Cholera Outbreak Eclipsing AIDS Crisis." December 10, 2008. www.irin news.org/IndepthMain.aspx?InDepthID=71&Report ID=81908.

43. Quoted in Médicins sans Frontières. "Cholera Outbreak in Haiti: Interview with Felipe Rojas Lopez, MSF Midwife," December 13, 2010. www.msf.org.hk/index.php ?option=com_content&view=article&id=1075:cholera -outbreak-in-haiti-interview-with-felipe-rojas-lopez-msf -midwife-&lang=en.

44. Barua and Greenough. *Cholera*, p. 24.

Chapter Four: An Easily Treatable Disease

45. Quoted in ScienceWatch. "Stephen Calderwood Discusses the Infectious Mechanisms of Cholera," July 2011. http://sciencewatch.com/ana/st/cholera/11julSTcholClad2.

46. Quoted in Rehydration Project. "Controlling Cholera." March–May 1993. http://rehydrate.org/dd/su52.htm#page5.

47. Quoted in Marshall. "In Bangladesh, a New Way to Fight Cholera."

48. Quoted in Jason Beaubien. "Can Vaccines Break Cholera's Deadly Hold on Haiti?" National Public Radio, February 7, 2012. www.npr.org/2012/02/07/145667552/can-vaccines -break-choleras-deadly-hold-on-haiti.

49. Pasteur Institute. "Dipsticks for Rapid Diagnosis of Cholera." September 9, 2003. www.pasteur.fr/actu/presse/press /03Cholera-E.htm.

50. Quoted in B.A. Foex. "How the Cholera Epidemic of 1831 Resulted in a New Technique for Fluid Resuscitation." *Emergency Medicine Journal*, September 19, 2002. http://emj.bmj.com/content/20/4/316.full.

51. Quoted in Joshua N. Ruxin. "Magic Bullet: The History of Oral Rehydration Therapy." *Medical History*, October 1994. www.ncbi.nlm.nih.gov/pmc/articles/PMC1036912/?page=31.

52. Joshua N. Ruxin. "A Sugar and Salt Solution for Haiti's Cholera Epidemic." *On the Ground* (blog), *New York Times*, November 5, 2010. http://kristof.blogs.nytimes. com/2010/11/05/a-sugar-and-salt-solution-for-haitis-cholera -epidemic.

53. Quoted in Rosenberg. "Saving Lives in a Time of Cholera."
54. Jon E. Rohde. "A Simple Solution." PBS, Spring 2005. www.pbs.org/wgbh/rxforsurvival/series/dispatches/a -simple-solution.html#author.
55. ICDDR,B.org. "50 Years of Cholera Research—Continuing to Save Lives." 2012. www.icddrb.org/media-centre/news /2143-50-years-of-cholera-research-continuing-to-save -lives.
56. Quoted in Ganapati Mudur. "Drug Resistant Cholera in India Attributed to Antibiotic Misuse." *British Medical Journal,* December 2, 2000. www.ncbi.nlm.nih.gov/pmc /articles/PMC1173496.
57. Quoted in Anne Mireille Nzouankeu. "Fear, Filth and Shame—Cholera on the Rise in Cameroon." Radio Netherlands Worldwide, December 16, 2011. www.rnw.nl /africa/article/filth-fear-and-shame-cholera-rise-cameroon.
58. Quoted in BBC News. "Haiti Mobs Lynch Voodoo Priests over Cholera Fears," December 24, 2010. www.bbc.co.uk /news/world-latin-america-12073029.

Chapter Five: Wash Hands, Boil Water

59. World Health Organization. "Frequently Asked Questions and Information for Travelers." www.who.int/topics /cholera/faq/en/index.html.
60. Quoted in Knox. "In Haiti, Bureaucratic Delays Stall Mass Cholera Vaccinations."
61. Rosenberg. "Saving Lives in a Time of Cholera."
62. Bono. "M.D.G.'s for Beginners . . . and Finishers." *New York Times,* September 18, 2010. www.nytimes.com/2010/09/19 /opinion/19bono.html?pagewanted=all.
63. Quoted in Water Supply and Sanitation Collaborative Council. "Global WASH Campaign." www.wsscc.org/wash -advocacy/campaigns-events/global-wash-campaign.
64. Quoted in UNICEF. "Community Approaches to Total Sanitation." www.unicef.org/innovations/files/CATS_field_note .pdf.
65. Quoted in UNICEF. "Community Approaches to Total Sanitation."
66. Quoted in Hayley Jarvis. "Children Taught Handwashing to Fight Cholera in Zambia." SOS Children, November 6,

2009. www.soschildrensvillages.org.uk/charity-news /archive/2009/11/childrenhandwashcholera.

67. Quoted in Gabrielle Menezes. "UNICEF and Partners Educate Children on How to Prevent Cholera." Relief Web, March 18, 2011. http://reliefweb.int/node/392637.

68. Quoted in UNICEF. "Community Approaches to Total Sanitation."

69. Matthew K. Waldon, Peter J. Hotez, and John D. Clemens. "A National Cholera Vaccine Stockpile—a New Humanitarian and Diplomatic Resource." *New England Journal of Medicine*, December 9, 2010. www.nejm.org/doi/full /10.1056/NEJMp1012300.

70. Quoted in Knox. "In Haiti, Bureaucratic Delays Stall Mass Cholera Vaccinations."

71. Quoted in Beaubien. "Can Vaccines Break Cholera's Deadly Hold on Haiti?"

72. Quoted in Tasha Sasaki. "Edible Vaccine to Revolutionize Medicine." *Highlighting Japan*, December 2010. www.gov -online.go.jp/pdf/hlj/20101201/28-29.pdf.

73. Quoted in ScienceWatch. "Stephen Calderwood Discusses the Infectious Mechanisms of Cholera."

74. Gerry Greenstone. "A Commentary on Cholera: The Scourge That Never Dies." *BC Medical Journal*, May 2009. www.bcmj.org/article/commentary-cholera-scourge-never -dies.

Glossary

antigen: Any substance that can stimulate the production of antibodies—particles that are part of the body's immune defense—and combine with them.

contagious: A disease that is communicable by direct or indirect contact.

deoxyribonucleic acid (DNA): The material that carries a cell's genetic information and hereditary characteristics.

developing country: A nation with an undeveloped industrial base whose citizens have a low standard of living, low life expectancy, and low education level compared to other countries in the world.

endemic: Native to or present in a certain location.

epidemic: A condition in which an infectious disease strikes larger-than-expected numbers of people in a certain locale.

epidemiology: The study of epidemics.

excrement: Waste matter discharged from the bowels.

global warming: An increase in the earth's average atmospheric temperature that causes corresponding changes in climate. Scientists believe global warming is produced by human activities such as deforestation and the burning of fossil fuels, which cause increasing concentrations of water vapor, carbon dioxide, methane, nitrous oxide, and ozone in the atmosphere.

miasma: Noxious vapors from decomposing organic matter.

microorganism: Any organism too small to be seen by the naked eye.

pandemic: An epidemic that occurs throughout a large region or even throughout the world.

public health: The science and practice of protecting and improving the health of a community.

quarantine: Strict isolation to prevent the spread of disease.

Organizations to Contact

Centers for Disease Control and Prevention (CDC)

1600 Clifton Rd.
Atlanta, GA 30333
Phone: (800) 232-4636
Website: www.cdc.gov

A U.S. federal agency that works to protect public health and safety. The CDC provides information on cholera prevention and responds to cholera outbreaks across the world, using its Global Water, Sanitation and Hygiene (WASH) expertise.

International Centre for Diarrhoeal Disease Research, Bangladesh (ICDDR,B)

GPO Box 128
Dhaka 1000
Bangladesh
Phone: (+88 02) 9840523-32
Website: www.icddrb.org

An international institution dedicated to saving lives through research and treatment. The ICDDR,B is one of the top centers for the study of cholera in the world.

Mekalanos Lab

Department of Microbiology and Immunobiology, Harvard Medical School
200 Longwood Ave.
Boston, MA 02115
Phone: (617) 432-1932
Website: http://mekalanoslab.med.harvard.edu

The Mekalanos laboratory is primarily engaged in the biochemical and genetic analysis of bacterial virulence factors. Its longest ongoing research project concerns the bacterium *Vibrio cholerae.*

United Nations Children's Fund (UNICEF)

3 United Nations Pl.
New York, NY 10017
Phone: (212) 326-7000
Website: www.unicef.org

UNICEF is an international organization that works to overcome poverty, violence, disease, and discrimination that affects children. It provides long-term humanitarian and developmental assistance to children and mothers in developing countries.

World Health Organization (WHO)

Avenue Appia 20
1211 Geneva 27
Switzerland
Phone: 41 22 791 21 11
Website: www.who.int

The WHO is an agency of the United Nations that is interested in public health. Its Global Task Force on Cholera Control was launched in 1992 with the goal of reducing deaths and addressing the social and economic consequences of cholera.

For More Information

Books

Diane Bailey. *Cholera*. New York: Rosen, 2010. This book focuses on the history of the disease, the steps taken to cure victims, and how cholera epidemics have shaped society.

Tina Kaufka. *Poverty*. Farmington Hills, MI: Lucent, 2010. The author examines the questions raised by complex issues such as globalization, the World Bank, hunger projects, the Millennium Development Goals, natural and human-made disasters, and many other realities of life in today's world.

Joseph R. Oppong. *Pandemics and Global Health*. New York: Chelsea House, 2010. Examines the impact of globalization on health and disease.

Internet Sources

Peter Bloland, Patricia Simone, Brent Burkholder, Laurence Slutsker, and Kevin M. De Cock. "The Role of Public Health Institutions in Global Health System Strengthening Efforts: The US CDC's Perspective." *PLOS Medicine*, April 2012. www.plosmedicine.org/article/info%3Adoi%2F10.1371%2Fjournal.pmed.1001199.

Bianca Moragne. "UT Biologist Discovers Source of 50-Year Cholera Pandemic." *Alcalde*, May 30, 2012. http://alcalde.texasexes.org/2012/05/ut-biologist-discovers-source-of-50-year-cholera-pandemic.

Angela Mulholland. "Misinformation the Enemy in Haiti's Cholera Battle." CTV News, October 30, 2010. www.ctv.ca/CTVNews/TopStories/20101029/haiti-cholera-misinformation-101030.

Pan American Health Organization. "Atlas of Cholera Outbreak in La Hispaniola, 2010–2012." http://new.paho.org/hq/images/Atlas_IHR/CholeraHispaniola/atlas.html.

Jorge Salazar. "Interview with Rita Colwell, Winner of the 2010 Stockholm Water Prize." EarthSky.org, March 29, 2010. http://earthsky.org/earth/interview-with-rita-colwell-winner -of-the-2010-stockholm-water-prize.

Deborah Sontag. "In Haiti, Global Failures on a Cholera Epidemic." *New York Times*, March 31, 2012. www.nytimes .com/2012/04/01/world/americas/haitis-cholera-outraced -the-experts-and-tainted-the-un.html?pagewanted=all.

UCLA Department of Epidemiology. "Who First Discovered *Vibrio Cholera*?" www.ph.ucla.edu/epi/snow/firstdiscovered cholera.html.

Abigail Zuger. "Folding Saris to Filter Cholera-Contaminated Water." *New York Times*, September 26, 2011. www.nytimes .com/2011/09/27/health/27sari.html.

Websites

John Snow (www.ph.ucla.edu/epi/snow.html). An excellent site that includes everything related to the famed epidemiologist— photos, a biography, a video of Broad Street, and more.

Medicine in 1860s Victoria (http://web.uvic.ca/vv/student /medicine/vicmedicine.html). Presents many of the medical techniques and treatments that were common in the 1860s.

Virtual New York City (www.virtualny.cuny.edu/index-2 .html). This site devoted to the history of New York City includes pages on the city's three cholera epidemics.

Index

Picture Credits

About the Author

Diane Yancey lives in the Pacific Northwest with her husband, Michael, and their cats, Newton, Lily, and Alice. She has written more than twenty-five books for middle grade and high school readers, including *Art Deco*, *Basketball*, and *Tracking Serial Killers*.